MEXICAN STYLE

MATT SEDILLO

FLOWERSONG
PRESS

Contents

What, to Chicanismo is the Poet?
What, to the Poet is Chicanismo?

Nolan L. Cabrera, PhD

The homie Matt Sedillo has done it again!

In his current collection of poetry *Mexican Style*, be prepared to go on a beautiful, intense, critical, community-oriented, wild ride. This work is socially critical of the numerous mechanisms of anti-Brownness and capitalist exploitation, while also being deeply introspective. It dives into celebrations of the culture while also finding parts of the culture problematic.

The through point is always the poet. It may be the poet lodging cultural criticism (e.g., *Ode to Calo*). It may be a poet celebrating *la cultura* (e.g., *Mexican Style*). It may be a deep introspective exploration (e.g., *I, Chicano* and *Sedillo on the Brink of Death*). Collectively, they challenge the reader to see the world through different eyes – eyes that both condemn oppression while also being honest about the inherent contradictions within our communities.

Reading this text, I was consistently reminded of Audrey Lorde's classic text "Poetry is not a luxury." Within this, she offered:

Poetry is not only dream and vision; it is the skeleton architecture of our lives. It lays the foundation for a future of change, a bridge across our fears of what has never been possible.

Here in lies the beauty and possibility of Sedillo's poetry. By doing the deep work within the community, his insightful vision engages the possibility and potential for a future that currently does not exist.

Sedillo accomplishes this with a deeply humanizing text, and it is also one that asks a lot of the reader. The allusions come fast and frequently. Even as a professor (by courtesy) in Mexican American Studies at the University of Arizona, I still sometimes had to rely on the University of Google to understand the depth of Matt's poetry (e.g., *The Assassinations of Ruben Salazar*). I mean this as a compliment, and a testament to the depth of this anthology.

One of the most striking features of this text is the boldness and courage to engage the full range of human experiences. While "LOL" is one of the most overused and misused terms in texting, I literally found myself LOLing in when reading the text like when Sedillo offered:

We didn't ask

To be born Mexican

We just got lucky

-*Taco Trucks, Every Corner*

Additionally, that poem spoke to a deep political engagement. The title came from "Agent Orange's" 2016 presidential campaign when his director of Latino outreach had the gall to say that a "Taco truck on every corner" would be the outcome if Hilary was elected - as if that is a bad thing!!! Flipping this ridiculous assessment on its head, Sedillo uses it as a way of envisioning a future where Brown folks are no longer minoritized. Within the poem, Sedillo lists the range of tacos available (Con asada, Lengua, Al Pastor, Carnitas, Cabeza, Chicharon, Cebolla y limon, Salsa y chile, Rojo y verde), making me hungry through cultural pride on the printed page.

This is the essence of Sedillo's text. There is humor coupled with searing social critique coupled with cultural exploration coupled with heartbreak. I was reminded of Cornel West's observation that, "Jesus weeps, but never laughs. Just like Socrates never cried." That is, many of our core archetypes of humanity are extremely limited in their range of human expression. In contrast, Sedillo's text boldly engages the full range of our collective Chicanismo – with all its tensions and contradictions.

He loves the community.

He is rooted in the community.

He is real about the community.

And

He is fiercely critical of White supremacy, capitalism, and colonialism.

For me, to poem *Mexican Style* is the center of the text. Engaging with Mexican boxing leading to Mexican work ethic leading to cultural pride was, to be blunt, brilliant. We are constantly told the contradictory messages: (1) Mexicans are lazy and (2) Mexicans are always stealing "our jobs" (whatever the hell that means). Through the metaphor of boxing, Sedillo unpacks how we as a people have a distinct style that is rugged, resourceful, and concurrently demeaned:

They speak of us as tough

But mindless

Hard working but barbaric

They disrespect our style

-*Mexican Style*

This style also runs throughout Sedillo's text while also not valorizing the community. In particular, he is critical of the competing self-aggrandizing forces that tend to work on behalf of instead of with the community. In a wildly complicated exploration (*Narciso's Cabin*), Sedillo is unmerciful (appropriately) on the constituencies weighing in on the community affairs (e.g., postmodernists, social media influencers, academics, lawyers, Marxists, etc.).

To develop this work, Sedillo is in constant conversation with community elders like *El Maestro* (*Ode to Calo, 1*) and the Old Man (*The Parable of the Track Runner*). Nowhere does this community wisdom shine through than in the poem *Yolqui*. This tribute to the recently departed Dr. Roberto "Cintli" Rodriguez – someone who was both a friend and colleague at the University of Arizona.

One of the most important challenges that Cintli collectively gave us was the charge for "creation resistance." Instead of simply resisting White supremacy, capitalism, and colonialism, he always said that we were compelled to envision and build alternative, liberatory futures. This ethic drives this poetry collection.

Yes, there are numerous social critiques.

Yes, there are internal community divisions.

Yes, the work is hard, but we are Mexican – hard work is in our DNA.

And therefore, we build. Through this building, Cintli's legacy is fomented:

So roll up your sleeves

And dry your eyes

Cintli lives

-*Yolqui*

This collective work, as Sedillo's poetry calls for, is a call to action, leading to a beautiful vision where the 45th's nightmare is our collective dream! I have offered my experience of this text, and I look forward to hearing yours, dear reader.

Enjoy the ride on which you are about to embark!

Peace,

NC c/s

Tinemiz Was Here

First up

Shadowbox

To break the dawn

Step, jab

Step back

Feint right

Check left

Hold the phone

Get low

Now dig to the body

Dig to the body

Dig to the body

Moves in silence

Jogs in place

In a house of four

Fast asleep

And slow to wake

In broken sweat

Palms his head

Freshly cut

Freshly done

Fresh from

The demands of each new day

Reaching for the next

Reaches for the machete

Reaches for the hatchet

Just for the backyard

Just for the cactus

Man of the house

Ever since the accident

 In a small town

Where everybody knew

That boy had hands

Throws breakfast on the counter

And cans and a blackbook on his back

And the sky has not yet fallen

And the mountains

The color of deep ocean

And the wind carries

All the dreams

 Of this place

That the light of day has broken

 And its red dirt roads are his

And its gray cracked forks are his

And the side streets, the back alleys

And all that there is here of heaven

Belongs to him

And if he could

He would take all that burns in this book

Pages of Nahuatl

Sketches of Calo

Older than his years

Bigger than his time

And bomb the sky

Of this town

This house

This life

That grows

Smaller by the day

Returns home

To the smell of fresh nopales

And a hot plate

To his name around a table set

To the averted eyes

Of his pregnant girlfriend

To his sister

Wheeling in on cracked linoleum

To his mother's lament

About a government check

That doesn't quite stretch

The way that it used to

To her clasped hands

Of undying gratitude

To the good lord above

For having sent the extra income

Of a good son

Who turned out to be a good man

Just like his father before him

And the sun has risen

Morning has broken

 Pack it in kid

The day has now begun

And it's round two

Round two hundred miles

To Los Angeles

Where his uncle

Currently lives

Same man

Who taught the kid

To slip a jab

To rack a can

That rivals dont rest

That nothing was handed

That any mark left

Would have to be taken

Same man

Who once taken away

Entrusted a name

Because he could not stop

Or outbox

 The demons within

And sometimes

Yes sometimes

When the kid closes his eyes

He can see him

In the distance

His uncle

Tio

Tocayo

Out in an ocean of mountain

Shadowboxing the night

And in that

Mystic act

They are one in the same

And in his fists

Live

Myth

Legend

Tradition

The ancient

The sacred

And if he could

He would take all that burns in him

And carve

Our legacy

Our lineage to the stars

So no one who came after us

Could ever mark us out

Or deny we were here

Throws an extra bag

A change of plans in the back

Could be a one way trip tells no one

Eyes peeled

 Hands on the wheel

In the driver's seat

Thinking long and deep

He recognizes the writers

On the trains

And he begins to dream

And when he dreams

 He is praying

And when he prays

He is dreaming

 Running and screaming

And the red dirt road Is sinking

Dear father

Who art dead and buried

Does anyone

Anywhere

Ever survive anything

Or are we all just passengers

To the end

Prisoners of guilt

Circumstance

And regret

Old man

How easy it must have been

  To have died young

  Before you could fuck it all up

Let them down

Walk on out

See how far your hands could carry you

  And by the time

  They reach Los Angeles

Twin Towers

Correctional Facility

Where his uncle

Currently hangs his head

No explanation is expected or given

  The prison is on lockdown

Guests are to be turned away

They will leave

  He will stay

Spend the rest of the day

  Out in front of that towering dungeon

Hoping against the odds

His uncle will catch a glimpse of him

Shadowboxing the dusk

Step jab

Step back

Feint right

Check left

Bob and weave

Cut the ring

Now dig to the body

Dig to the body

Dig to the body

Now dig to the body

Now dig to the body

Dig to the body

Dig to the body

Now dig to the body

Dig to the body

Dig to the body

That night he will seek out a trainyard

Fall to his knees

Close his eyes

And begin to dream

Of his mother

His sister

His lady

The child she is carrying

Of the story

He will one day become

Should he choose to run

And he will see

For the first time

He has spent

His whole life

Chasing fathers

Figures and shadows

That were never

There to begin with

At least not

The way we cast them

But none of that matters now

See we are myth

We are legend

And it is now up to him

To reach into this bag

And do right

With what he has been

Entrusted

That night he will sleep

In the park

Next day

Board a bus

Return to the family

He so deeply loves

And these trains will leave their station

Some ocean to ocean

Carrying the name

He was given

Tinemiz

Meaning you will travel

You will live

And the starlit skies are his

And the open plains

The cityscapes

The uptowns

The downtowns

The small towns

That live in canyons

The backs of yards

And the hillside villages

The east sides

The south sides

The west sides

The north sides

The roaring metropolises

 And all there is of heaven

Belongs to him

And anyone anywhere

Across this land

Where trains cross tracks

Could see

 That boy had style

That boy had hands

Pajaro

Pajaro, pajaro

Over land and sea

Pajaro, pajaro

Came to me

Pajaro, pajaro

Tell me what did you see

I saw our ancient name

Recovered

Through starry night, steam

Over metal sheets

I saw our righteous claim

Echo, chant and repeat

I saw anthems clash

I saw an old poet thrown

Into the gutter

In defense of the new poem

I saw courage on the troubled road

I saw our legend sung in a distant note

I saw the fire in our eyes

The wind in our lungs

I saw the pride we took

In the blood on our trunks

I saw a poet stare at the stars

In search of a wall

Pajaro, pajaro

Over land and sea

Pajaro, pajaro

Came to me

Pajaro, pajaro

Tell me what did you see

I saw the study of our struggle

Sold on open market

I saw a traitor guilt ridden

Drown in the river

I saw Cuactemoc in the cry of the Chicano

I saw us bond over the objects

We both once held

I saw our righteous struggle

Told against hostile city walls

I saw a people rise

I saw a hammer fall

I saw the cowardice of the Times

I saw as they poisoned the soil

Of our burial

Long before our birth

I saw the prison guards

Within us

Laughing

Beating

Running from memory

Of who we once were

Pajaro, pajaro

Over land and sea

Pajaro, pajaro

Came to me

Pajaro, pajaro

Tell me what did you see

I saw a poet

Work and whirl his way

To collapse

I saw the hunger for our story

Told to be told in white

I saw us bond over the lives

We never knew

I saw as the rich dined self satisfied

At our service

I saw a will wilt

In the desert

And a man change in a dream

I saw the enemy within

Dawn the mask of critic

I saw a man a stab at his father

Repeatedly

In pursuit of glory

Only to carry the wound

I saw a meme act in self defense

Teachers challenge a curriculum

Poets from a rooftop claim a city

Poets from suitcases claim a nation

Poets declare new holidays

Poets reach for a pen

Perchance to outlive

Time

Perchance to outlive

Death

I saw our ancient name

Return to the breath

Of all who heard it

I saw the falling sky

An east side protest

A quinceanera on

The sixth street bridge

We stood defiant

At the end of the world

Adelante

Open the borders

Smash the state

Abolish the prisons

Whose streets

Chale

This is our continent

No justice

No peace

No racist police

No officer

I am not happy to see you

I just got soup for my family

Aint no power

Like the power of the people

Because the power of the people

Don't stop

Say what

Aint no power

Like the power of the people

Cause the power of the people

Don't stop

Say their names

Sandra Bland

George Floyd

Breana Taylor

Tamir Rice

We're marching

For Black lives

Indigenous rights

Land Back

Free Palestine

Stop the pipeline

Water is life

Chale con

Nestle

Bechtel

Killer Coke

Yankee go home

Stop the bombs

Hands off

Cuba

Venezuela

Iran

The people

United

Can never be defeated

The people

United

Can never be defeated

To the political prisoners

Adelante

To the frontline workers

Adelante

To the teachers

Bus drivers

The food services

Fighting for their rights

Who would never cross that picket line

To anyone who has ever

Punched a clock

Pushed a broom

Worked a register

Walked a mile

In working shoes

This one's for you

Workers of the world unite

You have only your chains to lose

El pueblo unido

Jamás será vencido

El pueblo unido

Jamas sera vencido

El pueblo unido

Jamás será vencido

El pueblo unido

Jamas sera vencido

El pueblo unido

Jamás será vencido

El pueblo unido

(Unity clap)

(Unity clap)

(Unity clap)

(Unity clap)

(Unity clap)

(Unity clap)

(Unity clap)

(Unity clap)

(Unity clap)

(Unity clap)

(Unity clap)

(Unity clap)

(Unity clap)

(Unity clap)

(Unity clap)

(Unity clap)

(Unity clap)

(Unity clap)

(Unity clap)

(Unity clap)

(Unity clap)

(Unity clap)

(Unity clap)

(Unity clap)

(Unity clap)

(Unity clap)

(Unity clap)

(Unity clap)

(Unity clap)

(Unity clap)

(Unity clap)

(Unity clap)

(Unity clap)

(Unity clap)

(Unity clap)

(Unity clap)

(Unity clap)

(Unity clap)

(Unity clap)
(Unity clap)
(Unity clap)
(Unity clap)
(Unity clap)

(Unity clap)

(Unity clap)

(Unity clap)

(Unity clap)

(Unity clap)

(Unity clap)

(Unity clap)

(Unity clap)

(Unity clap)

(Unity clap)

(Unity clap)

(Unity clap)

(Unity clap)

(Unity clap)

(Unity clap)...............

Taco Trucks, Every Corner

Iron cast

Hand pressed

The heat

A pinch of salt

A cup of water

Masa de maiz

The steel

The bridle

The cactus

The eagle

The meadows

And volcanoes

A stone on the road

Destined to roll

The children of the sun

The people of the corn

We didn't ask

To be born Mexican

We just got lucky

This is the story

Of what has survived

What has endured

Centuries of rights

And doctrine

Discovery and conquest

De Landa and Cortez

Suns that set

And left us in complete darkness

Junipero

Pizzaro

Columbus

And other cannibals

This story began

Long before we met

But you don't know that

About anything

I mean you said it first

You said it best

America the beautiful

America

The exceptional

Pilgrim's pride

Each gain divine

Providence

The promised land

The sweet land

Of liberty

Opportunity

The free

Free land

Land rush

Guns up

Go west young

Manifest Destiny

Broken treaty

Empty promise

The Rio Grande

Is not Ellis Island

We will never be a part

Of your nation of immigrants

We will always be

Dirty Mexican

Good dead Indian

This is a story or recovery and restoration

Prophecy and legend

Eagle and condor

The flight

Of the butterfly

The return

Of the jaguar

Los Aztecas Del Norte

A peer reviewed socioeconomic study

On how block by block

Lot by lot

Reinforcements showed

Locked and loaded

Con asada

Lengua

Al Pastor

Carnitas

Cabeza

Chicharron

Cebolla y limon

Salsa y chile

Rojo y verde

Mas

Mas

Mmmmmaaaaaaaaassss

Caliente

You didn't ask

To be born when the Mexicans

Took

Back

Over

You

Just

Got

Lucky

Taco Trucks

Every Corner

Ode to Calo 1-6

Ode to Calo 1

The list

The light

The mic

The stage

Fathers and sons

Pride and regret

The final days

Hospital beds

The courage it takes

To be first

To say

I love you

I am sorry

The crowd laughs

They cry

They gasp

They sigh

At the young poet's command

Of hopes and dreams

Metaphors and motifs

The poet tears his chest open

Reaches for the stars

Is shot back down

One good night

Does not a legend make

Mighty tiendita

Legendary café

Shrine and furnace

Where legends are made

Heroes of the past

Mero meros of the day

Chicanos all

Shelved and weighed

By the gathering of dust

Splintered table

Forked staircase

El Maestro

Slams his fist

"We are in an undeclared

State of war

A culture war

A war of words

And ours must make advances

Onto the pages of the New Yorker

The Times

The Nation

And the Atlantic"

"Our words

Or yours cabron?"

El Maestro's rival interrupts

"Look listen

Shut the fuck up"

El Maestro

Quickly

Cleverly replies

Years ago

El Maestro

Had told once this rivel

On a panel

In an auditorium

Before peers

Professors and students

"Vato your poetry

Is so soft and sweet

I would call you the pan dulce poet

But even pan has substance

Even pan has

Some semblance

Of structure

Vato your poetry is like flan

You could cut through

It with a spoon

From here on out

You will be known as the flan man"

And since that day that label

Had haunted the poet

Readings

Signings

Gallery showings of important artists

The whispers

Followed

Even in the rival's most glorious moments

Some offhanded reference

Some underhanded dig

Would find its way from

The podium

From the lips

Of some unprincipled

Ambitious undergrad

In their attempts to climb up

By tearing down a great man

How the young tear at the old

How the future feasts upon the past

Blood on the flan

El Maestro continued

Having handled the would be

Insurrectionist

"We are the country's fastest growing demographic and it's least represented

We are several generations

Of our people's finest poets

And all we get from knowing each other is nothing

Is nowhere

All we do is bicker

All we do is tear each other down

Like el pinche flan man over there

Just look at him

Ridiculous"

With no one rushing to his defense

El Maestro's rival turns from the table

El Maestro continued

"We must pull our resources

Our access

Our networks

So their publications

Readings

Institutions

Become ours

We must stop fighting over crumbs

We must flood their spot

Have their kids learn our lingo

Our Calo

This is a cultural war

And either we become them

Or they become us

There is no other way around this"

El Maestro paused

For dramatic effect

"El hijo de azúcar

Flan man

Flanecito over there

Asked whose words

Would carry us

He asked out of shame

Out of ego

I ask what does it matter

Poetry is a public service

The point is not

Who writes what

The point is that

That the writing gets done

Once written

Poems have a life of their own"

At this

El Maestro was stunned

And silenced

By his own profundity

All applauded

Spare one

La Maestra

Young

Not for this world

But for this table

La Maestra said

"If we are as you say

At war

A cultural war

A war of words

Then why build up

The enemy's base

We must come together

Yes

But we must instead

Focus on what is ours

Build our readings

Our journals

Our institutions

There is work to be done yes

Chale con la chisme

La chamba si

La chisme no

Let us work

Let us work

On what is ours

Andale poetas

Adelante

Juntos

Let us build each other up"

The table began to applaud

As a history flashed

Before El Maestro's eyes

The mighty tiendita

The legendary cafe

When she first came

First took the world

By storm

How quickly

How deservedly

She did rise

How he wooed her

But for a short time

How their time together

Still lived in their exchange of hands

In her sad glance

How now he could feel

The table turn

El Maestro thought

Of his agent

La gringa

La gavacha

What power shift

Was she after

She put this idea

In his head

Convince the others

Chicanos should take over

White institutions

Who had ever heard of such a thing

She knew it would fail

How could he have been so stupid

She had set him up

But had there been collusion

La gringa

Was after all

All of their agents

How deep did this betrayal

Go

But why

El Maestro's eyes

Began to water

And with that his rival

Turned back to the table

And in joy and delight

Exclaimed

"Everyone look

El Maestro is crying

He is crying

Ja ja ja

Look look

Mira mira

The big man is crying

You can't take it

Everyone look

El Maestro is crying

He can't take it

You can't take it

You're crying

You're crying"

Ode to Calo 2

And that night

That night

Like any other

El Maestro

Walked bottle in hand

The old

Neighborhood

The storied blvds

The emptied streets

The cherished placita

The lonely park bench

His eyes dart and drift

Turn to the work

Of painters and sculptors

Masters of their craft

Masters of another time

Masters some

Who had died

Some who said

Their work was in

Conversation with his

But where were these words

To be found

Nowhere in print

What was legacy worth

In stone

In in paint

In text

When they could all so easily be

Shelved and discarded

Whitewashed and forgotten

How precarious

Our legends sit

In the palms

Of each generation

El Maestro wept

And wept

And wept

Pled his case

To murals and plaques

To the heroes of the past

"How could those levas

Back at the cafe

With their pretentious

Overpriced conchas and cafecitos

With their wretched poems

Of floricantos past"

Not see the genius

Of his plan

El Maestro

Fell into a memory

Into a nostalgia

Into a summer

A summer

Like no other

He 50

She 36

The fall

How she swore off

All poets

After him

How relieved he was at this

How much more

Could one poor heart take

El Maestro

Looks to the stars

Looks to his palms

"What are memories worth

When life is always changing"

The old man

Stumbles back

To an apartment

Filled with awards

Clippings

The gatherings

Of the man

He once was

Rests his head

Wondering what is left

But on this night

This night unlike any other

Once his eyes close

His mind races

And all the stories

The memories

Of everyone

He has known

Swirl

Condense

Caramelize

Into his own

Writing

In murals

Collages

Homage

Pastiche

Loteria

Heroes and villains

El Maestro

El Borracho

El Valiente

Who will fight

For la luna

Las estrellas

The hand of

La dama

La Maestra

And now he is

Timeless

Ageless

Unborn

And

Ancient

The hopes and dreams

The metaphors and motifs

The voice of many generations

The old poet leaps from his bed

Pen in hand

Blank page attacked

With the words

Chente

Lucha

Chavela

A mighty tiendita

Fathers and sons

Pride and regret

The courage it takes

To be the first to say

I am sorry

I was wrong

On this night

On this night unlike any other

El Maestro

The old master

Rises above his ego

Rises above his shame

Drafts an epic

An anthem

An ode

To the people

Calo

Then drifts back to sleep

Ode to Calo 3 `

Like You
I Am Joaquin

Still I Rise
A Dream Deferred
Una Rosa Blanca
The beating heart
Of movements
Revolutions
The masses
The millions
And on this day

This day
Unlike any other
The poet is sure
He has written such a poem

A poem

That shares an author
With the sun
The mountains
The legends
We all knew
Before we were born
The poet's eyes scan

His apartment

Shrine and tomb

Of all his achievements

Open mic to feature

Feature to author

Author to awards

Awards to curriculum

Curriculum to lifetime

Achievement

All shallow and dim

In the light and depth

Of this newly written poem

The poet eyes

His desk

The poet eyes

His pen

The poet's eyes

Drink in

His notebook

The poet's life carries him

And there the poet finds

Nothing

Nothing

Absolutely nothing at all

The poet flips through the notebook

The poet seeks torn pages

Counts the pages from the book

Matches the page to the count of other

Blank notebooks

The poet's hands tremble

Horrified

The poet falls to the floor

Terrified

The poet crawls into a corner

Mortified

The words had gone missing

The words were nowhere to be found

Those words

In perfect order

Unlike any other

Were missing

It wasn't a dream

It wasn't a mistake

This was a living nightmare

A day terror

El Maestro was sure of it

Someone must have broken in

Someone must have replaced the notebook

With an identical one

This was the only

Rational explanation

Poems don't just leave the page

El Maestro was sure of it

The poet's mind raced

Through his extensive

Mental rolodex

Of enemies of the people

Cross checked against

Access to his apartment

It was obvious

How could he have been so naïve

How could he have be he so stupid

It was that pinche vieja

That wicked witch

That old woman

The landlord

And her worthless drunkard son

El Maestro stormed from his room

To the halls

Up the staircases

Dressing as he rushed

Bang

Bang

Bang

At their worthless door

Demanding answers

The woman cried out

"You're late again

You lousy bastard

You are late on your rent

And I have to suffer for it"

The poet cried back

"Pinche slumlord

Enemy of the people

Where is my notebook

You cannot steal a man's work

As collateral

You don't know who

You are messing with

I will rally the tenants"

At this threat

The door flung open

The drunkard son seized El Maestro

Pulled him into the apartment

And without warning

Lifted the old man

Over his head

In a fireman carry

Began to spin

And spin

And spin

In dizzying circles

As the landlord clapped and laughed

Quick thinking

The old man held onto his pants

As one shoe and his hat fell to the ground

The young drunkard set

The old poet down

Lightly shoved him about

Laughing as El Maestro

Regained his balance

And reached for his shoe

And his hat

El Maestro fled

As the drunkard son

Warned next time would be worse

His mother still laughing

El Maestro vowed revenge

But was certain

These two mamones

Could not have stolen the poem

To the tiendita

El Maestro assumed his seat at the cafe

Sure the enemy was near

The flan man was holding court

Taking notice of how

Uncharacteristically quiet

El Maestro was being

And in his rival's eye

El Maestro saw the look

The unmistakable

Look of knowing

But what did the flan man know

And what did the flan man merely

Suspect

And did he know

This thing

That El Maestro now also knew

How could he not

Any rival worth having

Knows when their rival

Also knows the thing

That both rivals know

But neither rival will say

Lest it tip the balance

Of the rivalry

El Maestro was sure of it

La Maestra

Made her way to the table

El Maestro broke from the poets

Asked her to walk with him

La Maestra agreed

Once they left the café

El Maestro

Began to tremble and shake

Preparing for what he had to say

And said nothing till they reached the park

La Maestra worried

The old man was dying

At the sight of his nerves

El Maestro

Told her about his dream

The rush of words

How sure he was

That wrote this poem

In a dream

But in reality

Woke up and wrote it down

Before drifting back to sleep

That this poem

This poem

Calo

Was one for the ages

His finest work

At this advanced age

His once last chance

To stamp his name as one of the greats

The true greats

Beyond Chicano fame

The kind

That are talked about

Centuries after their death

La Maestra relieved

Smiled and said

"Our poems

Are dreams"

La Maestra

Left El Maestro in tears

On a lonely park bench

Head held in his trembling hands

El Maestro

Bargains

With the murals

Pledges his life

To write nothing

But odes to Morelos

Makes the same deal

With Lazaro Cardenas

And Pancho Villa

Should the poem

Find it's way back

To his desk

The walls

Their plaques

Their murals

The memory

The past

The legends he knew

Before we were born

The ones

That shared an author

With the sun

And the mountains

El Maestro speaks

"My poem

That poem

Was never mine to begin with

It was written

By all of you
By all of us
And one night
With or without my hand
We will write the poem again"

Ode to Calo 4

Just as sure as the sun will rise
It will surely set
Just as seasons pass
One generation to the next
A heart string
A window to the soul
A train of thought
Ideas come
Ideas go
And all one can hope
Is to come across
A few
Worth of hitching a ride
Worth finding your life flashing
Outside
The raging windows
Cut the strings

This is the train

Get on the train

El Maestro's eyes

Scanned his apartment

A good run

One for the ages

Mighty tiendita

Legendary cafe

Shine and furnace

Where legends are made

Chicanos all

Shelved and weighed

By the gathering of dust

In the past few months

El Maestro

Passed the baton

To

La Maestra

And as the Chicano famous poets

Shared and shared alike

Their work found new audiences

Old wounds healed

And they all moved forward

Juntos, together

And El Maestro

Knew some kind of happiness

Until the day

His rival

Flanecito

Rushed into the cafe

Waving papers

The New Yorker

The Times

The Atlantic

And the Nation

The first poem

Ever to be published

Simultaneously

In all of them

Written

By a mystery Chicano

The splintered table

Demanded the poem

El Maestro's mind raced

His heart sank

As the flan man

Began to recite

Words familiar

Of a people

A pueblo

A love

A loss

Fathers and sons

An anthem

El Maestro

Did not think

El Maestro sprang to his feet

"Those words

In that order

That poem

Is mine"

As the table cried

"Shut the fuck up carnal

And listen to the poem"

El Maestro lunged at the flan man

Grabbed him by the collar

"This vato finally lost it"

Laughed back the old rival

As El Maestro was pulled off

El Maestro grabbed the

New York Times

And ran into the street

Enraged

In tears

La Maestra thought to run after him

But as the flan man

Continued reading

From the Atlantic

La Maestra was moved

By the poem's beauty

El Maestro's mind

Scrambled

And his eyes melted

As he read the lines familiar

The words torn from his notebook

All pressed against the pages

Of the New York Times

All the words fit to print

He searched the poem

For an author

To find the thief

Only to find

The contact information

Of la gringa

La gavacha

His agent

The poem

Had an agent

This poem had

The same agent as him

The same agent

As all of them

Of course

El Maestro called

Enraged

It was as he always suspected

La gringa had stolen

His poem

"You thief"

El Maestro cried

As the agent laughed uncertain

The accusations flew

Until finally she responded

"You know that I love you

But your claims are outrageous

If I wanted a poem

About cars on the lawn

Or flying chanclas

You are my man

But this poem

This poem is unlike any other

You chicanos have ever written

It captures

The real essence

The spirit

El sabor

Of your people

You could never"

"How did you get a hold of this poem"

El Maestro screamed

"The papers all reached out

Assumed I was the poet's agent

Look, listen

When you are calm and ready

If you already know who it is

Introduce me to the real author

And I will book you

As the opening act

This poem

Is already taking the world by storm"

"You're fired"

Cried El Maestro

"You can't fire me

I made you

I'll replace you

You will regret this"

Cried back La Gringa

And the phone clicked

And just as sure

As the sun did rise

And the sun did set

Time did pass

And El Maestro

Was asked

To give up his seat

For a rising young poet

Who wrote exclusively

On fathers and sons

Pride and regret

Mentorship

And the lack thereof

El Maestro did not fight

Day for night

Night for day

A bathrobe and cereal

Alone in the apartment

Waiting on death

Until the day El Maestro heard

The poet behind the poem

The poem

That had taken the world by storm

Would make his first televised appearance

El Maestro heard

They brought Charlie Rose

Out of retirement

As it was said

He would strike the right balance

Between public recognition

And intellectual credibility

Just the right man

To introduce this

This new grand master

Of American letters

To the new American public

Reshaped now

By the poem's existence

And there on the day

There Charlie Rose sat

At Charlie Rose's old desk

And there before an audience of millions

Charlie Rose said

"I am here with the poet"

Before interrupted

"Charlie I really must stop you there

You see Charlie

I am not a poet

I am a poem"

And there sat peeking out

A brown tweed suit

The words that had indeed

Left the page

The words that had the cut

The strings

That had left the station

There before the millions

In all it's beauty

One for the ages

The poem itself

Free now of the poet

Calo

Ode to Calo 5

Mighty Tiendita

Legendary Cafe

Tourist attraction

Where t shirts

And mugs are sold

And profit is made

In short time

Since the publication of

Calo

Ethnic studies bills

Began to pass

In every state

Hollywood was put

Under a consent decree

And forced to represent

The country

As it actually exists

With up to date statistics

From the pew research center

Calo

Was a cultural phenomenon

Calo

Was an unstoppable icon

Calo

The first poem

Invited to dine at the White House

Calo

The first poem

To throw the opening pitch at the opening game of the world
series

Calo

The first poem

To host back to back episodes of Saturday Night Live

Though the second appearance

Was not without controversy

As the poem's opening

Monologue

Calo strongly criticized Lorne Michaels

For his abysmal history

On Chicano talent

The audience gave Calo a standing ovation

Calo was after all

A poem of the people

In Calo

La gringa

La gavacha

His agent

Saw all her dreams

For the Chicanos

Finally realized

In Calo

The flan man's

Career saw

A resurgence

As a loyal friend

And opening act

Flanecito

Saw the world

Reading his new inspired work

In Defense of Flan

Critics said his best work

In decades

In Calo

La Maestra

Found inspiration and passion

Deeper meaning

And wider distribution

Diego and Frida

Simone and Jean Paul

Caló y La Maestra

One for the ages

The poets returned

To the old neighborhood

Spoke at its

Largest auditorium

Standing room only

The audience

They laughed

They cried

They gasped

They sighed

At the poem's command

Of metaphor

And motif

Hope and dream

During q and a

A familiar face

Appeared from the crowd

Coughed and trembled

Pled into the microphone

"You know the truth

You are my poem

I am your author

Come home

To the notebook

All will be forgiven"

The flan man seethed

La gringa seethed

La Maestra turned her face

Calo stood

"I am Calo

Old man

I know you not

But it is true

You are my author"

Calo paused for

Dramatic effect

The crowd gasped

None but El Maestro

Knew what would happen next

El Maestro knew the poem's

Basic use of dramatic pause

El Maestro had

The poem's timing down

And headed for the door

Calo continued

Before the silenced crowd

"I am Calo

Anthem to my people

All Chicanos are my author"

The crowd stood in ovation

As Calo continued

"I am Calo

The anthem of Carnalismo

Calo champion of my people"

And as many in the audience

Openly wept

As others shouted in outpour

Of uncontrollable emotions

El Maestro had already left the building

Sat in the gutter

Waited for the flinging

Open of doors

La Maestra

Rushed at

And cursed El Maestro

For his ridiculous claim

That she alone

Knew the truth of

El Maestro said nothing

La Maestra pled

To return to la gringa

La blanquita

To join them

On world tour

La Maestra

Reminded the old man

He was once a legend

El Maestro turned from her

As he had turned from the applause

Left La Maestra in tears

Returned to his apartment

Filled with clippings

And notifications

Of awards

Not of his own

But of the poem's

The poem

Calo

The anthem

Calo

The false hero

Calo

The vendido

Who claimed to be

Of the people

But only ever sought

The approval

Of white institutions

Calo

The villain

Calo

The usurper

Calo

The corruptor

Calo

The assassin

El Maestro

Knew what must be done next

El Maestro was sure of it

Ode To Calo 6

A light

A stage

A panel

The press

Their outlets

The academy

The practical machinery

Of legacy

Four chairs

Two poets

One agent

One living poem

Four chairs

One table

One night

One calendar date

One year of immortality

El maestro

A wig

And a mustache

Unrecognizable

Incognito

Dressed as wait staff

Calo steps into the light

"I am Calo

Anthem of the Chicanos

Calo

Beacon to my people

Calo

The living embodiment

Of all your hopes and dreams

Calo

Shaped by your hand

Your imagination

Calo

Shaped by history

Calo

The shaper of history"

The crowd sat in silence

In awe

At beauty and dignity of Calo

Spare a lone voice

That cried out

"At long last

Why don't you

Shut the fuck up

Cabron"

El Maestro

Pulls a revolver

From his coat

Prepared to kill

His creation

His reflection

His naked ambition

All achieved without him

But instead stood frozen

For the first time

Silenced and mesmerized by

The beauty of Calo

La Gringa

Cried out

The flan poet

Cried out

La Maestra turned away

The security guard

Threw El Maestro

To the ground

Dragged the old man out

Broken from the trance

El Maestro screamed

"No

No

No

You don't understand

I am the poet
I held the pen
I alone wrote
The poem"
Calo
Roared in response
"I am Calo
Anthem of my people
I have no single author"
Security
In his mid to late 50s
His father
In his final days
So much
Left unsaid
Until they read this poem
This poem
Alone
This poem
Calo
That spoke
To their hearts
To their fighting
Spirits
To years of silence
To decades of pride

To silent regret

This poem alone

Allowed strong arms

To let down their guard

If only for a moment

The security guard

Like millions more

Would kill for this

For this poem alone

With no single author

El Maestro

Removed from the building

Thrown into the gutter wept

"You don't understand"

The security guard

Lifted El Maestro

To his feet

Dusted the old poet off

Embraced him

And quoted

His favorite lines

From his favorite poem

"Get it together Cabron

Once written

Poems have a life of their own"

Three Kings

This poem is based on a true story

Partially

Some of it

And the rest

Well the rest is up to us

Now let us begin

Out there

Out where

Out on the interstate

Through valley and canyon

Where dynamite

Long ago split the mountain

Out where big rigs

Carry big business

Blood money

With even bigger interest

Blood on the highway

Blood on the roots

That connect field to factory

Desert to metropolis

Eyes

Ears

Mouths to market

Out where everyday

Without complaint

We single file

In four to six lanes

Tooth and nail

Hammer at the hip

All ready to pin our sweat to the economy

Out here

Where we swallow our tears

In this concrete field

Of deadened dreams

Is where I caught a vision

A vision of three kings

Laughing triumphant

Majestic in crisis

One at the hood

One at the wheel

One waving the shirt off his back

That red and black checkered flag

With no time to wait on CHP

Triple A

Or Caltrans

Badges

We don't need no stinking badges

I saw three Mexicans in the middle of the freeway

Directing mid-day traffic

And I imagined

The troubled roads

The vultured skies

The hardened paths

That harden hands

In these troubled times

The sun

The sand

The heat

The tar

The gravel

That these proud men must have traveled

To make possible

This roadside miracle

That smog fueled parable

Three kings with rolled up sleeves

Facing the road together

Out on the edge of forever

Out on that expressway to nowhere

Where billboard stretches as far as they eye can see

All selling the promise and the dream

The plot and the threat

The best laid plans

Of mice and men

Of sweat and strain

Like rats in a maze

Out here

Where everyday

We show our teeth

We sharpen our glare

Hiss at the oncoming traffic

And out my windshield

In the distance

I could see it

A grand mirage arising

In place of a horizon

Bloodshot and gridlocked

Spellbound and hellbent

The people

Just look at them

All fucked up

And paved in plastic

Right to left

East to west

Into certain death

Into the gaping jaws of the highway

They just kept driving

Into nine to fives

That ate them alive

Graveyard shifts

That tore life from limb

Into the belly of the beast

The feast

Of the very cannibals

That feed

On our blood

Our sweat

Our tears

Our hopes

Our dreams

Our fears

Our cowardice

Our compliance

And that's the true crime

The real tragedy

What are we so scared of

We're dead already

And in the distance

I could hear the men singing

A song of redemption and resistance

Revised for our purpose

And true story it went something like this

We three kings

Have traveled this far

Carrying this economy in our strong arms

Through fields and canyons

Mines and mountains

Now get in the fucking car

And I could hear us

Joining chorus and verse

On that proud day

When the tables finally turn

When the first shall be last

And the last shall be first

Hands of struggle

Hands of might

It's the working hands

That make these cities bright

It's the means were seizing

Still proceeding

Now guide us in our righteous fight

And we set fire to the highway

Reduced billboard to ash

Pulled the rich from their beds

Their slumber from their sheets

Pressed their faces to fields of cold concrete

And I swear upon the troubled road

I could hear them cry

I could hear them scream

As we took back all they had stolen

All their lives

And it was right

And it was just

And this poem is based on a true story

Possibly

And the rest

Well the rest is up to us

Huelga

There was something

In the water

The winter

The wind

This proud old man

His grandkids

Their friends

Same thing

In their city

Their country

Their region

Their land

The culture that unites us

The legends that bind us

Their immortal flag

That served as reminder

That legends

Legends

Are only legends so long

As they are retold

Gather young

Children

Gather around

The old man

Cried out

For a tale told

Of the days of wine

And roses

Poetry and explosives

Molotov and manifestos

When men and women

Of flesh and blood

Lived and loved

Across the pages of history

And the comrades

Cried out

Huelga

Huelga

Huelga

And the workers

Cried loud

Huelga

Huelga

Huelga

And the students

Cried proud

Huelga

Huelga

 Huelga

Huelga

Now children

This

Story is best told

In the reading of two letters

Hers to him

We are not the first

Nor shall we be the last

Should we die

In struggle

Let the comrades

Tell our families

We are sleeping

Let them take us

To highest peak

Let the snow fall upon us there

Now his to her

Light flashes

Darkness stretches

And our moments

All too fleeting

The trenches

The frontlines

The general strike

Should we die

Then let it be as we lived

Huelga

Comrade

Huelga

Huelga

Mujer

Huelga

Huelga

Amor

Huelga

And when he returned

They died

As they lived

Then lived on

On banners

On placards

On a logo stamped

A photograph

An immortal flag

Two comrades

Storming the barricades

And the workers

Cried out

Huelga

Huelga

Huelga

And the comrades

Cried loud

Huelga

Huelga

Huelga

And the children

Cried proud

Huelga

Huelga

Huelga

Huelga

Danzante

Latch key kid

Mom teaches

Dad makes

Another man rich

Stomping

Screaming

Family name

On the building

The owner's son

Pushes his finger

Into his worker's chest

"Says English

Do you speak it"

Right in front of the worker's kid

Kid's father trembles in silence

2006

Home alone

Latch key kid

Television set

Latch key kid sees

A young boy with a drum

An old woman chanting

A cholo with a flag

He sees Aztecs dancing

He sees the newscast tremble

He sees the mayor tremble

He sees the experts on TV tremble

A fire lights

As something in him awakens

But when he tells his parents

They say those people

They are not like us

That night his rage will burn in him

Unable to sleep

And she has seen everything

The moratorium

The walkouts

Prop 187

SB1070

Immokalee

Sensenbrenner

Given her life to the movement

The wind of her lungs

To her people

Tells her granddaughter

About an action at Pershing

Says is it is a shame

No one even knows to be offended

Talks the expedition

Talks the revolution

Villa

Diaz

The Magon Brothers

Who wrote right here

In the city of Los Angeles

Talks about all our history

That goes without monument

Her granddaughter

A torrent of rage

A storm of self hate

Disconnected from time and place

From people who lived and died

For something

Her granddaughter speaks loud

But says nothing

Wants nothing

To do with anything

Mexican

And he swears

By creator

Danza saved him

That before

Life was a roaring river

Drowning in addiction

A halos of bullets

In the city of angels

But he has put that all behind him

Traded attire

For atuendo

Mota

For copal

Senseless violence

For the strength and wisdom

Of warriors and prophets

For the rivers of Mexica

Blood coursing through his veins

Chilanga born

East LA based

Only problem

She says she has with Chicanos

Is that she thinks they take themselves

Way too seriously

That and that

They are always searching for

Something

Some ceremony

Somewhere else

Like they can't feel

The Earth beneath their feet

Like for them

Mexico is some kind mountain

Made up of dead Indians

Not something alive

Adapting

Just trying to survive

Just like them

But she never tells any of them

Any of this

Because

They are her friends

And they remind her of home

And she is here for a good time

And when times get rough

For the good fight

And from all four directions

They come to dance

For parents

And grandkids

So whitewashed

And stupid

They don't recognize

Their own reflection

From the four directions

They dance to remind us

That it is never

To late

To reconnect

To who

We have always been

With the fire

In their eyes

With the wind in their lungs

With rivers of blood

Coursing through their veins

With the strength of mountains

They dance

For El Paso

Adam Toledo

Vanessa Guillen

For missing

And murdered

Indigenous women

To dance

Down the walls of the geo prisons

To free the children `

May the border wall fall

May the towering prison

Crumble

May the lying newscast

The wicked politicians

May their murderous police

May their murder cities

May the enemy tremble

At the sound of our drum

Mexican Style

"He only fights Tijuana cab drivers"- Greg Haugen

"I am going to punch him in the belly

See how many jalapenos he has down there"- Greg Haugen

"Aint one hundred thirty thousand Mexicans

That can afford tickets" - Greg Haugen

"I am going to tear your head off"- Julio Cesar Chavez

Mexico City

February twentieth

Nineteen ninety three

Azteca Stadium

One hundred

And thirty four thousand

In attendance

Hands high

Elbows tight

Inside

Outside

Mid range

Cuts the ring

Smothers the guard

Angles off

Left hook to the liver

Short straight right up top

Chavez KO Haugen

Round six

"We have a saying in Mexico

We don't fuck around

I fight for honor and glory

Nothing else"

Canelo Alvarez

"Hey no Max

I fight Mexican style

Gennady

Triple G

Golovkin

"Golovkin says he fights Mexican Style

But tonight

He is using his Eastern European skills"

Max Kellerman

Between nineteen sixty eight

And two thousand twenty three

The country of Mexico

Has produced one to six

World champions in the

Sport of boxing a year

One hundred sixty one in total

Two hundred and twelve

If you count the Chicanos

And yet time

And time again

Our skills are called into question

They speak of us as tough

But mindless

Hard working but barbaric

Rugged but unskilled

They question

Our skill

Because they question

Our intelligence

They question our intelligence

Because they mean

To work us

They mean to work us

Like beasts of burden

Then call it unskilled labor

They make religion of it

Their faith

Unshakable

Because their economy

Depends on it

But it takes skill

And it takes intelligence

To work the fields

The factories

The canneries

To load the trucks

Stock the shelves

Do the electrical

The plumbing

The landscaping

Under the table

There is no such thing

As unskilled labor

And there is no such country

That produces

Hundreds

Of world champions

At something they are not good at

And if there is such a thing

As a Mexican style

It is roll with the punches

You can't see coming

It is to split seconds

Into decisions

"I would argue that a Mexican Warrior

has heart, passion,

and fights until the very end

with intuition and intelligence.

A Mexican warrior

will not die

in the line

of fire,

but will cunningly

be

three steps ahead" Canelo Alvarez

In the build up to the rematch

Triple G

Repeatedly challenged Canelo

To stand in front of him

And fight like a Mexican

Then spent the whole night backing up

Because he could not handle the pressure

So with all due respect

Either side of the border

Check the stats

Hardest working people on the planet

And with all due respect

And in a sport defined by its toughness

We are known as the toughest

Los mas chingon

And with all due respect

I take great pride

In the fact

That I bring all that I am

To all that I do

My heart

My will

My determination

But also my skill

My mind

And my imagination

Just like I wrote

This fucking poem

Mexican Style

As of Late When I Look to the Stars

When I was a kid

My father taught me to play chess

And then never let me win

How to throw a punch

Not to lunge

To secure position

Control the center

Use misdirection

After the laughter

The tears

The reconciliation

After the last glass shattered

After I was certain

Everyone was fast asleep

I would sneak

From my bedroom

Crawl through my window

And stare at the night

So far and wide

So indifferent to the troubles

Of my sad, sad little life

To the constellations

I'd brag and boast

The man I'd become

Once strong and grown

For I knew even then

That life came

In waves

In chapters
In acts

That this too would pass

So I did not cry

Or bow my head

When I got word

The stars were dead

That their reflective light

Was but a measure of time

The record of what once was

No I vowed young

To live my life

To live and die

A star

Portrait of an artist

As a young retail associate

Ahead of my time

Nineteen

And already a failed

Playwright and novelist

Arrogant

And insecure

The uncrowned prince

The dirt

In the belly of a worm

At work

I would stare at the clock

Contemplate my mortality

My obituary

Here lies a man

Who folded shirts

At night

I would drink the poison

Down the hatch

Bitter with all creation

Plot my self destruction

Hang in there kid

All the world's

A stage

Just not yet

And these days as of late

I live my life

Staring from the windows

Of airports

Hotels and planes

At the stretched lit sky

So far and wide

So indifferent

To the triumphs of my sad little life

And these days

As of late

When I look to the stars

I wish only for rain

To wash away

The weakest

Most arrogant, insecure

Parts of me

Till that is left is a link

In a chain

That extends before

And after my death

A link in a chain

That I'd wrap

Around my fist

Find a wall

And swing

And swing

And swing

Until I

Or it falls

Because we are all gonna die

We are all gonna die

It just seems like

In the meantime

You ought give

Your life to something bigger

You know

Ignore Them, They're Lopez

When choosing the right man

For the job

Why not consider yourself

A Lopez

A Lopez

Is Sturdy

Reliable

Economic

Hard working

God fearing

And one day

God willing

A Lopez is going to change the way this country works

Yes sir

OSHA violations

Forget em

Labor laws and regulations

Why sweat em

It's industry standard

It's a cold hard fact

For projects big and small

Once your company goes Lopez

You'll never go back

And if by some off chance

You get some off brand

Loud mouth

Wild eyed

New age

Blue haired Lopez

Asking questions

Making demands

Just pretend they don't speak English

Oldest trick in the book

But still effective

Otherwise next thing you know

You got a goddamn Lopez march on your hands

And trust

When I say no one wants that

No sir

The birds to the sky

The fish to the sea

And the Lopez to work

The Lopez was born to serve

Why else would they be so good at it

And if by some off chance

The cries and pleas

Of the Lopez grow

All too desperate

All too human

For you to continue

To ignore them

Just have someone else talk about it

Then have them change the subject

How bout Ellis Island

The 1800s

Race in America

Then cover everything under the sun

Except the people working hardest under it

And when the Lopez finally gets it

When the Lopez finally sees

That their silencing

Is the key to the oppression

When the Lopez

Finally makes their play

For greater representation

In film

Print

Television

News

And academia

Or any other way a country

Explains itself to itself

Then and only then

Listen

Really listen

Take notes

Call your notes

Field notes

Ethnography

Get your friends in on it

Call your friends peers

Cite each other

Call what you write

Peer reviewed articles

Start a journal

Call for submissions

Conferences

Objectivity

Call your subjects

Lowps

Do it so often it becomes

Industry standard

Lowps studies

Now you're ready for your close up

You'll need an agent

An assistant

A full time make up artist

 For your many televised appearances

Promoting your latest work

American Lowps

Where you explain to the American public

How a group of people

Could get so used and beaten

Battered and exploited

Murdered and discarded

And then be so quickly forgotten

In towns

Cities

Counties

All

Called Lopez

Officer Mendoza

Sick of this town

Sick of her parents

Sick of the ready

Acceptance

Of unspeakable

Evil

Soon off to college

Soon off she

Has promised

To make all of it

A distant memory

Border town

Border Patrol

Never talks politics at work

Never takes his work home

"They are throwing kids
In cages"
His daughter cries out

"They are throwing kids

In cages

Kids that look like you

Kids that look like me"

Her mother demands silence

Haunted by silence
Haunted by sleep

Haunted by the river's call

Officer Mendoza

Thinks of the company

He keeps

Of the monsters

They have all become

The monsters

They have always been

Haunted by sleep

Haunted by dreams

By the river's call

You will know rest
You will know peace
He sees his wife

His daughter

His parents as children

Wade in the water

He sees himself

In a guard's tower
Years ago he saw
A man crossing over
Shot in the back

Just last week
He read of a mass grave

Of bodies buried in the desert
He thinks of the unknown
The untold

The unclaimed
The river

Its power

To wash away his sins
Haunted he sleepwalks

His way to the river

To the water
Finds there a woman
Dressed in all white
Crying for her children
The disappearance of
Officer Mendoza

Remains a mystery
The whereabouts of his remains
Unknown

Cuauhtemoc

Five o clock

Alarm

Goes off

Five ten

Five fifteen

Five twenty

Five thirty

Six ten

Oh shit

Hit the shower

Hit the road

The 60

The 605

Traffic light

The 210

The 134

Traffic jammed

Side entry

Brick building

Slam the door

Slam the door

Slam the door

The fund drive

The looming sale

The desperate measure

Heavy is the head

The Literary Director

The National Coordinator

The CEO and CoFounder

The Poet Laureate

Of struggle

The Best Political Poet in America

The lead host

Co hosts arrive

Five minutes to show

The theme song

The red light

"Welcome to la raza radio

Radio for la raza

La causa

Radio para la gente

De Aztlan

Radio for the people

We at La Raza Radio

Are here to raise

The voices of the pueblo

And forward an analysis

Rarely heard on the airwaves

We draw our understanding

From the study of history

And economics

And our sense of direction

From the demands of the people

And the movement

Join us for an hour of insight

Strength and dignity

Join us for an hour of Chicano

Power

Chicana

Power

Chicanx

Power

Welcome to La Raza Radio"

And from Santa Barbara

To Tijuana

Over the airwaves

Over Pacifica

Vanessa Bustamente

AKA Homegirl Doctora

The first Chicana

National chair

Of La Raza Unida

Her voice raised high

In a life

Of firsts

And she is just getting

Started

Conferences

Keynotes

Inspirational speeches

Block booking

The college circuit

Broadcast

Podcast

Makes the most every chance

To break

Down a door

To lead the way

To make a space

For Brown kids

In places

They were told they did not belong

Ernesto

Ernesto Ayala

Aka Ernesto Ayala

Reads the community

Calendar

This week in Aztlan

Matt interrupts

"Where but KPFK

Will you hear these voices

Where but KPFK

Will you hear

These announcements

This analysis

At this hour"

Vanessa makes the pitch

"If you value

What you're hearing

Call in

Get on the line

818 985

KPFK"

Later that day

All three are booked for an event

Vanessa will make a speech

Table her merch

Matt will recite poems

Sign some books

Ernesto

Ernesto Ayala

Born and raised

And to this day

A man of Pacoima

Second generation

La Raza Unida

Man of the people

Backyard a graph yard

Living room

A study group

A war room

A national treasure

A library

Of national liberation

Ernesto

Ernesto Ayala

Takes the mic

"When the Spaniards came

They destroyed

Our temples

Cut our tongues

Changed our names

But we drove them out

Renamed the land

In the name of our ancestors

Mexica

Mexico

And

The Americans

With their cannons

With their rockets

Red flare

Their sirens still blare

Under the color of law

Their reign of terror

They hunt the young

Rob us

In the light of day

But all is not lost raza

Teach your children

What is theirs

Teach your children

We have been here before

Teach your children

We have fought

Teach your children

We have won

That it is always darkest

Before the dawn

Teach your children

That in their ancestors name

The sun will rise

Not long from now

Soon

Some day

In a place

They will call

Aztlan

Bandolier

Sugar skulls and marigold

Mezcal

Papel picado

Pictures

Posters

Postcards

Photographs

Books of scrap

What we struggle to remember

What we long to forget

What we use

What we choose

What we lose

What we discard

And what we keep

To remind ourselves

Who we are

Who we've been

Who we long to be

A candle lit

She lifts her glass

Throws one back

A toast proposed

To the ancestors

But only the brave ones

Never the cowards

To fighting spirit

Past and present

To family legend

And the horse it rode it on

To a tall tale

Told her when she was but a child

By her mother

A letter

Written by a man

Bandolier clad

With hands of leather

His blood

Still running through their veins

Sending for salt

Liquor

Tortillas

And gunpowder

When she was young

She would conjure the dust

Cup the proud echo past

And walk hand in hand

With heroes of the revolution

Their storied lives

Still strengthening her bones

Though sometimes

When the sun shone bright

She would reach for still living ghosts

Phantoms

Absence

Her father

Traitor

Coward

Deserter

Hardly worth the mention

So she rarely did

Instead she raised herself a clenched fist

Un grito

Howling down the avenue

The oldest of two

Her brother's keeper

Side by side

They'd ride

The back of the bus

Guarded

Guided

Protected

By spirited battalions

From another time

And together they never were alone

Calacas y calaveras

Altares y fronteras

La lucha y ofrendas

Hopes

Dreams

Visions

Promises

Life

Time

Sacrifice

Moving boxes

Town to town

Job to job

The same old song

The same cruel markers

Hitting the same cruel notes

Their clothes

Their mother

Her accent

A bloody nose

A right cross

A left hook

A broken jaw

Now this is the part

Where they learned to fight

Where they kept their pride

Where their mother taught

If anyone made fun of them

Or told them to go back to where they came from

Well

Then they had their mother's permission

To send those devils back to hell

And that is the story of how they grew up rich

On odes and corridos

Leyendas y dichos

Sangre y antepasados

The skin of their teeth

The marrow of their bones

Why so long as they had one another

They feared nothing

And called each other home

Now this is the part

That still makes her cry

Darkens her door

And stretches the night

Shoots stars from the sky

And scars her eyes

In the shape of what she longs to forget

A napkin sketch

A family crest

Her brother has penned

Been six years since

And still none of it

Made any sense

His only charge

Was all he ever had

His pride and a clenched fist

Resisting arrest

He'd been resisting his whole life

Tonight

The apartment is a mausoleum

And her mother a flickering flame

All but extinguished

And all the pain

All the same

All too great

So all this time

They kept their distance

On nights like this

There is no strength in memory

No glory in the past

Just the simple fact

That the world is so much bigger

And stronger than any of us

That we were just born

On the wrong side of a losing war

Nothing more

Than her brother had lived

That her brother

Had fought

That her brother

Was here

That her brother

Was strong

That her brother

Was proud

And now her brother

Is gone

On nights like this

On nights like this

The room spins around a candle lit

As in her tightened grip

She holds her next step

Breath

The bottle

The pill

The ledge

And the sky hangs low

And the clouds close in

On candles on a corner

Laces on a wire

A constellation of street light vigils

When they were young

They would conjure the dust

Cup the proud echo past

And bend time

From the back of the bus

And with each stop

The world against them would weaken

Pachucos and Adelitas

Braceros y Magonistas

Would climb aboard

Drafting plans y corridos

And the driver was

Un grito de guerra

With the command of cannons

And hands of leather

And in those days

They feared nothing

For nothing was dead

And all they remembered

Lived in them

And on nights like this

Time like this poem

Collapses in

Calacas y calaveras

Altares y ofrendas

Sugar skulls and marigold

The streets fill with ghosts

The city is ours

Now this is the part

Where she sees her brother

As he was

As he'd been

As he is

As we are

Timeless

Sacred

Heroic

Soldiers

In a war that never ended

And never will

Until the day

We win it

A toast proposed

To the ancestors

For they are we

And we are them

To the land

And those who work it

To those who chose

To die on their feet

Rather than live on their knees

Light a candle for me

Keep it in your heart

Make me an altar

Until we meet again

Always remember

Be brave

Stay strong

For in each other

We are never alone

This Poem

This poem

This poem

Is for Boyle Heights

Lincoln Heights

El Sereno

East Los

City Terrace

Where neon memory

Lights rivers of concrete

Where an avenging eagle descends

Where Vanessa Guillen

And Miguel Hidalgo

Loom large

Where

Las calacas de Posada

Ward off

The ghoulish dreams of realtors and developers

Where the blood of Salazar runs

Red Mosaic

Where at long last

The Blue Demon

Silences Trump

In a chokehold

Of justice

This poem

Is for

Santa Ana

P Town

Pacas

Barrio Logan

The Mission District

Where sacred winds

Set the invader adrift

Where the music never died

And Richie still lives

Where las Adelitas hoist

La Bandera

Where Frida

Holds up the pillars

Of a highway bridge

Where machine made men

Of white death

Sign our foreclosure

This poem

After Denver

Burque

Tucson

San Anto

El Chucho

Pilsen

Little village

Where the blood money took flight

Where we declared our imagination

Where Trumpty Dumpty

Fell from a crumbling wall

Where a two headed hydra groped

An instrument of death

Where our mothers

Sisters

Daughters

Restored

The stars

To the corn

Where we decried the war

Where the nuclear heart

Of empire

Radiated our bones

This poem

This poem is not for

Whitewashing

Gentrification

Career politicians

This poem is for

America Tropical

Where revolutionaries

Cross centuries

To confront enemies

Old and new

For the Mexican

Cultural

Institute

Of Los Angeles

Give us back our keys

This poem is for Tenochtitlan

Where I learned to write

Before I learned to think

Where I first saw histories collide

American rail lines

Spanish cannons

Blades of obsidian

Revolutionary smoke

Maximilian

Cortez

Diaz

All condemned

One breath

One stroke

When the fire in the eyes

Of

Cuauhtemoc

Benito

Hidalgo

Zapata

First lit

The dormant torch

In mine

I was fourteen years old

When I first saw

Diego Rivera's

History of Mexico

When a mural

First changed

My life

And this poem

Is for our beautiful people

Our righteous struggle

Our glorious past

Our brighter future

Now and forever

Mi tierra

Mi lucha

Mi gente

Mi sangre

My gift

This poem

This poem

This poem

This poem

This long delayed poem

Ahora y para siempre

Que viva la raza

I, Chicano

A Chicano poet

Sits at a desk

Attempts to pen

An anthem

A classic

A grand sweeping epic

Of economics

Demographics

The fear of a Brown nation

On a bronze continent

The motive engine

At the beating heart

Of the Mexican Question

The Chicano condition

Now somehow lost

In land of confusion

American neurosis

And Hispanic

Serving Institution

A Chicano poet

Sits at a desk

And attempts

To dive into ink

Into parchment

An open letter

An honest ledger

Of wins and losses

Martyrs

And marches

The Mothers

Of East Los Angeles

Crusades for Justice

Justice for Janitors

The Justice 8

Los Siete

De la Raza

The Boulder 6

The Vasquez Rocks

The Silver Dollar

A Chicano poet

Sits at a desk

And attempts

I, ranchero

Vaquero

Bandito

Goro Blanco

Bracero

Pachuco

Brown Beret

Inmate

Cholo

Vato loco

Pocho

No sabo kid

Son and heir

To all I have seen

But been taught to forget

The crimes they commit

Then omit from the text

How they changed the law

When they stole the land

How they taught our kids

They held no claim

Took up too much space

Had to change their names

That they had come a long way

To nowhere

I saw a Chicano poet

Sit at a desk

And attempt to pen

A hope

A dream

A prayer

May I spend my days

And nights

Scouring the archives

Of a lost tribe

That stitched together

Every thread of history

And culture they could find

And called it home

May I carry the movement in my heart

Where my heart on my sleeve

And enshrine our heroes

In these poems

I, Corona

Acuna

Tenayuca

Caesar

Dolores

Gomez-Quinones

The plan de Santa Barbara

San Diego

Catalina

La Tierra Amarilla

I, Tijerna

Alurista

LRU

UDB

CSO

ATM

A rifle

And a press

A pen

And a sword

Yes I, Flores-Daniel Gang

Y Flores Magon

Yes I

500 years

Then I

500 more

I, Betita

Cortina

Jovita

Modesta

Moreno

Barrera

Cabrera

Ayala

Carrasco-Cardona

I, Munoz

Muniz

Ruiz

La Raza

La Cronica

Regeneracion

Yes, I lucha

I sique

I Cintli-Rodriguez

I return

To the corn

I, Corky

I, Joaquin

And I look the same

And I feel the same

And I have survived centuries

Of genocide

And war

Racist politicians

Right wing militias

Pseudo intellectual academics

Calling our good name into question

I, Movimiento

Estudiantil

Chicano

De Aztlan

And I shall endure

El Martillo

Yo soy el martillo

The hammer

The builder of bridges

The destroyer of walls

And you shall greet me as a brother

Or you shall come to know me

By the hammer's fall

You have the right to remain silent

Miranda vs Arizona

1966

You have the right to an attorney

Escobedo vs Illinois

1964

The Thin Blue Line

A phrase popularized

By then LA

Police chief

William Parker

Following

An incident wherein dozens

Of drunken officers

Rained their violence

Upon caged Mexicans

But you have never heard of

Ernesto Miranda

And you have never heard of

Danny Escebedo

And you have never heard

Of Bloody Christmas

Greasers

Or the issue of Spanish

And Indian blood

Can be disarmed

Committed

Sentenced

To hard labor

The Greaser Act

1855

Where suspicion exists

Without warrant

An officer may arrest

A person if they are believed

To be alien

SB0170

2010

Between the 1840s

And the 1870s

Mexicans were lynched

At the highest rate

Per capita

Of any group

In American history

In 2019

A man drove

Hundreds of miles

To kill as many Mexicans as possible

In the 1930s

Then President Hoover

By some estimates

Deported a third of our population

Sixty percent of them

US citizens

In the 1950s

Under operation wetback

President Eisenhower

Left hundreds of Mexicans

To die in the desert

To drown in the ocean

And the economy was booming

Good times

Bad times

There is always time

To round up the Mexicans

Mexico will poison us

Ralph Waldo Emerson

1846

If you don't want to be killed

By Isis

Don't go to Syria

If you don't want to be killed

By a Mexican

There is nothing I can tell you

Ann Coulter

2015

What has miserable inefficient

Mexico to do with peopling the new world

With a noble race

Walt Whitman

1846

When Mexico sends their people

They don't send their best

They're bringing crime

They're bringing drugs

They're rapists

Donald Trump

2015

Cambridge Analytica

Called the Trump campaign

Project Alamo

His hate rallies crescendoed

With the chants of

Build the wall

And Mexico will pay

We been paying for

Centuries

For whatever

It is

That they imagine

We did to them

At the turn

Of the 20th century

Arizona and New Mexico

Became states

Only after reaching

What the federal government

Deemed to be

A suitable white population

At the turn of the 21st century

The population share

In every state

Of the so called non-Hispanic white

Is on the decline

Ours is on the rise

Today

7 out 10

Of America's biggest cities are located

In the southwest

In the land that was once Mexico

Today

The most common age

Of the so called

Non Hispanic White

Is 58

Ours is 11

One has grandchildren

One will have them

The battle has been won

The decisive blow has been struck

And though I may never live

To see it

I will build the bridge

I will destroy the wall

Yo soy el martillo

The hammer

The Assassinations of Ruben Salazar

East LA

1970

August 29th

Signs of the times

"Indians of all tribes"

"Che is alive

And walking down Whittier Blvd."

"Be Brown Be Proud"

"Chale con Nixon"

"Brown Is Beautiful"

"Chicano Power"

"Chicano Means Power"

"Tierra Y Justicia"

"Somos Chicanos

La Raza de Aztlán"

"Nuestra lucha está aquí"

"Ya basta

No mas"

"Stop killing us"

"Our fight is in the barrio

Not Vietnam"

A bridge

A river

A column

A reporter

A war

A murder

A cover up

An investigation

A moratorium

A police riot

Hit pieces

Redactions

The assassinations of Ruben Salazar

August 29th

1970

Califas Aztlan

Five percent of the country

Twenty percent of the dead

Thirty thousand deep

In the streets of East Los Angeles

A war abroad

A war at home

The pigs

The dogs

The gas

The batons

Believing he is being followed

Salazar

Ducks into the silver dollar

Deputy Wilson

Stalks Whittier

Salazar

Ran a column for the times

Two cousins

Mexican

Dead

A police murder

A slow investigation

Every reason to believe

There was a cover up

Wilson approaches

Ruben has joked

What this movement really needs

Is a martyr

Once wrote

Of bridge and a river

Ruben takes his life in hands

Every time Salazar lifts his pen

Deputy Wilson lifts his rifle

Is it time

Is it near

Is it done

Must the measure of a life

Always be weighed in blood

Deputy Wilson fires his weapon

Ruben is struck

Salazar is dead

September 15th

1970

Los Angeles

California

The inquest into death of Salazar

Sticks

Stones

Broken windows

Posters of Che Guevara

District attorney's

Only interest

And there is every reason

To believe

There will be a cover up

September 15th

1970

Occupied America

Where they shoot the messenger

Then the question the photographer

Where they kill a man

Then name a park in his honor

Where every military occupation

Requires the character assassination

Of the people living under it

Where murderers redact

Their own documents

Where cowards sit in an office

Where a man once stood

Then run

For decades

With lies

Is it August 29th

Is it September 15th

Is it 1970

Is it 1846

Is it 1492

Is it 1519

Is it the same day on repeat

Is our fight still in the barrio

Is Brown still beautiful

Is Brown still beautiful

Are they still killing us

Are they still killing us

Ruben

Are they still killing us

Does Chicano still mean power

Nuestra lucha sigue aquí

Northern Harvest

South by southwest

Texas is the cruelest state

Pedro's mother

In her dying days

Tells her son

The man he believed

To be his father

Was not

That his father

A bracero

Died

In a town called Wasteland Texas

In the last year of the program

A list of instructions

A set of names

A death bed

The day after Pedro buried his mother

Pedro boarded a bus

To find the truth about his father

Many names

Buried and dead

Lit with hatred

The faces of the living

None would speak to Pedro

And the days

Into weeks

And his stay

Grew eerie

And angry grew the stares

Of the town of

Wasteland Texas

Angered by silence

Pedro grabbed an old

And frail man

Shook him forcefully

Frantically

"Clearly

My father was a scoundrel

I have not come to Wasteland Texas to defend him

But to know

Tell me

Tell me now

Tell me who I am

What were the sins of my father"

Finally in terror

The old man spoke

"There is no use in unburying the dead"

Pedro threw the old man to Earth

Still in search of the sins of his father

Pedro heard

The voice of a stranger

"You will not find your father

Shaking what little life

There is left in old bones

Nor will you find him

In your still young strength

My name is Jorge

And your father

Was my father

And I alone can take you to him"

Pedro as he was told

Followed Jorge

Out of the town

Down a dirt road

Nearing a home

A small home

With darkened windows

Pedro rushed ahead

Of his half brother

Towards something

Somehow familiar

Near the home

Pedro saw a tree

A tree he could not remember

Against the tree

Laid a shovel

Pedro turned to Jorge

Jorge held a gun

Pedro did not miss a beat

Pedro cried

"If you are to kill me

Then kill me

But first tell me

Something of value

Something I can use

Before I die

Tell me who I am

Tell me

What were the sins of my father"

Jorge paused

Reflected

Then spoke

"Man is born

Man seeks cause

But man is weak

Man is flawed

And to you the shovel

And to me the rod

It is written here

In our father's law

You will not unsteady my hand

Lest our positions

Reverse

Now take this shovel

Be of use

And get to digging"

Pedro dug into the night

Into deep rich soil

And the deeper Pedro dug

The more transparent

The roots would become

Until the roots were completely clear

And in them Jorge could see

The flashing images

Of his life

Then the life of this town

Racing too quickly

To make sense of them

Racing too quickly

To derive any meaning

Pedro kept digging

To Jorge's armed laughter

Pedro dug and dug

And he dug and he dug

Until the soil collapsed

Into a town

The town of his father's sins

Surely here he would get the answers

He was seeking

He was welcomed

He was fed

He was bathed

He was clothed

He was told

Not to ask about his father

There they knew mercy

There they knew peace

The type Pedro had never known

Insatiable Pedro persisted

And persisted

And persisted

Until town's cheerful tone turned grim

"Ask again and you will share your father's fate"

Pedro knew these kind people

Had murdered his horrid father

But why

Jorge laughed

"You will have to dig deeper that"

So Pedro dug

And he dug

And he dug

Past still more transparent root

Pedro dug

And dug

And dug

Until he heard the shouts

Of the people below

And Pedro thinking himself a hero

Cried back "hold on"

Pedro dug forcefully

Frantically

And the shouts increased

Growing louder

The harder he struck

Until finally the roof caved in

Until Pedro crashed into an office

There he saw an old time press

And the headline read

"Your Father is Dead"

"Impossible" Pedro cried

"I was born

In 1964

Final year of the Bracero Program"

A woman turned to him in scorn

"Your father

Had a father

And your mother

Had a father

And they had fathers

And none of them wanted you

You are the bastard

Of a northern harvest

Now get over it

Take these papers and distribute them

They are killing our people"

The woman was Jovita Idar

And the year was 1915

Pedro did as he was told

Pedro took to the streets

With a sense of purpose

Texas was lynching Mexicans

We had to fight

We had to resist

But once the papers were distributed

Once again Pedro was lost

Pedro wandered the streets

And came upon a church

The church of the dead

He entered the mass

As the preacher in the pulpit

Read from the book of fathers

"Life is the maddening crowd

Dog eat dog

A crab reaching for the sun

But I filled my bucket

With blood

Seek not my sins

My son

Forge your own path"

And with that Pedro leaped from the pew

Cried out

"How can I know who I am

If I do not know the sins of my father"

And with that

The doors sprung open

His half brother Jorge

Rushed upon him

Pulled him by the ear

And out of the church

And out of the town

Back down

The dirt road

To the family tree

Back into the hole

Cast down the shovel

And to the digging commanded his brother

And Pedro dug

And dug

And dug

Until the earth collapsed in

And Pedro found himself in yet another town

The town of women

Failed by the broken

Promises of men

And everywhere

Was pain and lament

And tales of woe

Cruelty, violence and abandonment

Pedro in tears

Pleaded with the women

Begged for forgiveness

And asked what he could do

They told him he could be a good man

And presented him

With a transparent root

He grabbed hold and he became another man

A man who clearly drank

His wife

Crying before him

He called in the children

And promised never again

That he would be

A good father

A good husband

A protector and provider

A good man

That he would never again

Lift his hand

Lest to work

And time passed

And Pedro forgot his brother

His mother

His father

The transparent root

Pedro worked the fields

Times were hard

And the fields filled with poison

One day he came home

Telling his wife

He planned to organize

And she said

"You used to talk like this

When you would drink

When you would beat me

And the kids

You used to talk like this

You need to keep your promises

You need to be a man of your word

You need to be a man of work

You must sacrifice

Without complaint

You must protect

You must provide"

That night

Pedro dreamt

Of the Salt of the Earth

And the scene where Esperanza

Says "I just want to rise

And take everything with me"

And Pedro thought

"Oh to have such a woman

Oh to have such a redemption arc"

And just then the door swung open

Jorge pulled Pedro from his bed

As Pedro pretended to be upset

Leaving his year as a good man

Jorge walks Pedro through field of pesticides

Jorge began to weaken

Pedro held his half-brother up

Until they reached the dirt road

Where Jorge regained his strength

He threw Pedro

Back down the hole

"Getting to digging you fool"

And now no longer

Afraid

Pedro digs with purpose

Of his own

In search of a cause

And Pedro

Dug and he dug

And he dug

And he dug

Until he saw a transparent root

Until he saw men

At the border

At the checkpoints

At the turn of the twentieth century

Were being doused with poison

Pedro grabs ahold of the root

Now surrounded by his fellow workers

In a warehouse

Stripped naked

Sprayed with DDT

Pedro cries out

"We cannot allow this

We are men

Not animals

And this poison

Is not fit even for animals"

And with that

A group of men

In need of work

Begin to beat Pedro

Mercilessly

To silence him

Pedro back in the dirt releases

The root

And begins to fall from the sky

Free again

Of his father

His brother

His mother

Some broader struggle

In this time he decides

That whatever is left

Of his life

Need not be a response

To anyone

Pedro closes his eyes

And tells himself

"It is time that I decided

Who I am"

But when Pedro opens them

The year is 1938

And the Pecan Strike

Is on

Emma Tenayuca

Rallies the crowd

Emma leads the march

The moment is electric

Pedro joins it

And suddenly once again

Pedro's life has meaning

Purpose

A way forward

Until Pedro surround by struggle

Again realizes

That while he knows

What he must do

He still does not know who he is

So Pedro leaves the march

Leaves the strike

Walks down the old dirt road

Where there he sees

The old house

The old tree

Where the old shovel

Once rested

In its shade

Jorge laid against it

Behind the house

Pedro buries his brother

Marks his grave

And beyond it

Sees an arrangement of stones

And a plaque with some engravement

Pedro turns his head

Heads back down the hole

And digs

And digs

And digs

Pedro sees in the transparent root

The massacres

The rangers

The suffering of our people

Pedro sees himself as an Indian

On Spanish Hacienda

Pedro sees the rise and fall

He sees a city built upon a lake

He sees an eagle slay a snake

He sees all that came before

He sees all that came after

And just then

Pedro realizes

He has been dead

For a very

Very

Very long time

And with that grabs hold of a transparent root

And with that returns

As a grape on the vine

Pedro sees a small plane in the distance

And with that realizes

At long last

Who he is

He is the seed

The soil

The root

And the crop

What he is not

Is the sin

That poisons

The harvest

Buendia

Off the grid
Out in the sticks
There are boxcars
In the desert
Where no one
Stays long enough to live
Ask the how
Why
What
Where and when
They just try to make the best of it
Out here
These days
Trying to make the best of it
Is the closest
Anyone ever gets
Half town
Half myth
The road to Buendia
Is littered not paved
By the cat and mouse
Of billboards
And track homes
That never came

Spare a single model

On a single lot

Just in case the market

Ever does pick back up

Say they want to build a prison out here

But they're going to have

To find the place first

Buendia is a city on the move

A town of the future

An unincorporated fugitive

That cannot

Will not

Be pinned down on any map

State or federal

That's how they get you

Last checked

Buendia had more doctors

Per capita

Than any place on the planet

With the birds

The people of Buendia

Would laugh and sing

Grow crops from windows

Whisper their lineage into trees

Round midnight

The fireflies of Buendia took the sky

And an orchestra of crickets

Stirred the stars

Commanded the night

In the town

Of Buendia

There are no half measures

No mayor

No city planner

No city council

Just a gray haired elder

With a silver beard

Entrusted to teach

Each generation

Of the sandstorm

Born of a hummingbird's wings

Of the sandstorm

That carried the first families

That carried the boxcars in

That the drifters

Were their guests

That being of service

Gave life purpose

That purpose

Was never a burden

Always a gift

Then against the town's wishes

The elder

Taught the children

To cast stones

At the model home

For shining and glimmering

The outside world was a threat

Half real

Half magic

Half surreal

Half tragic

The town of Buendia

Is old and breaking down

And by the time

Construction begins

And the boxcars go out

The track homes come in

And the crickets are silenced

And the doctors and fireflies

Go their own way

And for the first time

A changed name

Appears on a map

One day the keeper of the flame

Tells a group of children

The legend of the wind

The children begin to laugh

And cast stones

The town goes all in

And everyone lives in a track home

And everyone works at the prison

And every night

A new prisoner

Howls in his cell

And every night

The door opens

And a gray haired elder

Appears dead and bloodied on the floor

And every night

A new prisoner

Is beaten senseless

And taken to the hole

And every night

A new prisoner

Threatened with extended

Sentence

As silence is demanded

And every night

In the low light

Of the prison yard

Of this makeshift graveyard

The guards of Maldia

Correctional facility

Do what it is that they do best

Shovels in hand

They bury each night's memory

Alongside the rest

Before returning to

Their families

Their televisions

Their homes

Their codes of silence

Before they do their best to forget

Because these days

Out here

Silence

Silence is the closest anyone

Ever gets

Sedillo on the Brink of Death

Write

As you memorize

Memorize

As you write

Practice

In the car

"Sugar skulls

And marigold"

Write as you memorize

As you write

"Sugar skulls

And marigolds

Mezcal

Papel picado

Pictures

Posters

Postcards

Photographs

Books of scrap"

A poem about death

"Books of scrap"

"Books of scrap

What we struggle to remember

What we long to be forget

What we use

 What we choose

What we lose"

Memorize

As you write

Practice

In the car

Self imposed deadline

The size of the legend

Determined

On what is done in life

Must finish

The manuscript

"Sugar skulls and marigold

Mezcal

Papel picado

Pictures

Posters

Photographs

Books of scrap

What we struggle to remember

What we long to forget

What we use

What we choose

What we lose

What we discard

And what we keep

To remind ourselves

Who we have been

Who we are

Who we long to be"

Memorize as you drive

As you memorize

Practice in the car

"Sugar skulls

And marigold

Sugar

Sugar

Sugar sku

Sugar

Sug

Sug"

Words stuck

Face numb

Drive a blur

A hospital rush

Insurance quandary

Hand shaky

Brain fog

Mind rush

Mind rush

Rush mind

Can't focus on

 Insurance

On commerce

Rush to triage

Stupid questions

Pain on scale

Scale one to ten

Stupid questions

Struggling nurse

Needles

IVS

Poke for the vein

Brain stuck again

Air bubbles

Air bubbles

Worry

Worry

Worry

Air to the heart

Death

Hallway

Deathbed

Or slumped in a station chair

What does matter

Deathbed

More dignified

Mind drift

Mind race

Someone cut the brakes

Doctor finally seen

Asks

"Have you been

Experiencing unusual

Levels of stress

As of late"

And I think

This man is stupid

And I think

This man is an idiot

I think stupidity

Is a kind of death

So long as I am some kind of brilliant

I am alive

I just need

Need

Neeeeed

To focus

To discipline

To focus on discipline

To work harder

To bring value

To my name

To put words

To paper

That someone will remember

After I'm dead

That and that alone

Brings value to life

I cannot be convinced otherwise

Memorize

As you write

Or the crowd will fade

"Sugar skulls

And marigold"

We are three

We are

We are three

Three of us here

Here in the hallways

Woman is crying

Very distracting

"Mezcal

Papel picado"

Woman is trembling

Woman is lying

About drugs

About the drugs

She has clearly taken

Which she says he has not

I am sure of it

I can hear it in her voice

I can tell

Doctor agrees

Doctor says "I am not the police"

Doctor says "if you're not honest

I cannot help you"

Woman admits to drugs

To consumption

To addiction

To illegal narcotics

I get the sinking feeling

She should not have done that

I am relatively sure of it

At this hour

Her condition

Almost everyone is the police

I am sure

She will bring the law upon us all

I have not done anything wrong

I am sure of it

I worry one day the law

Will be the death of me

A man in sleeping in gurney

A man is sleeping in a hallway

Half conscious

Half asleep

All alone

His son is worried

I hear

His son is out of state

The hospital wants the old man out

I can hear it in their voice

Why are they talking so loud

Why can't any of us get a room

This is all very distracting

I must focus

I need to focus

Must focus

My

My

My mind

I am wheeled away

Laid out on a table

My body fed

Into a cat scan

Into radiation

Radiation

My head examined

Technicians

Say "relax"

I try to narrow my focus

Make narrow the stress

Focus on something else

I close my eyes

I close my eyes

I close my

I crash into a dream

The car flies

Over an overpass

Into a field of lights

The end is near

I'm going to die

I hear my father's voice

"Son

Son

This is important

Son

If you can hear me

Do not cry

They will know

If you cried

You carry our name

You have carried it further

Than any of us

Don't let your tears

Outlive it"

Wheeled back

Wilt in chair

Pull phone from pocket

Email half finished manuscript

"If I die

Publish this

Send my regards

To my father

And my royalties

To my mother"

Face numb

Head pulse

Scramble to finish

"Sugar skulls

And marigold"

Insurance returns

Insurance insists

I am in better

Condition

To answer questions

To conduct

Business

The business

Of health care

Police stalk the hallway

And the woman cries

And I think she was right

Not to trust the doctor

I begin to distrust the staff as well

The old man is shuffled out

Into the parking lot

Alone I guess

My paperwork arrives

Stress they say

Stress is the culprit

Relieved I look to the world

Around me

I recall the crying woman

I begin to imagine

A story of addiction

Of cruelty

Of this system

That would cage

That kind of hurt

I think of the old man

I think of the worried son

I think of the hard decisions

I think of no one

Really wanting to leave

I think of the capital

That comes between people

I think of families

Torn like this

I think of last rites

Untold in the cold concrete

I think of all we readily accept

In the parking lot

In the parking lot

I look to the stars

I think

Of manuscripts past

Recall the chest pains

I confused for cardiac arrest

The ulcers I confused for sepsis

And now a pulsing migraine

For a stroke

This is the stress

This is the toll

Memorize

As I drive

Drive as I memorize

Memorize

As I write

A poem

About death

Practice in the car

Burn into my memory

"Sugar skulls and marigold"

The Mexicans /Even When We When They Speak of Crisis/No Pigs in Vato Heaven/Fort Hollywood (A Semi True Story About a Semi Real Place Sometime Called Los Angeles)

The Mexicans

Referred to

Only as the Mexicans

At gunpoint and British accent

A group of men

Are ordered

From the back of a kitchen

Pulp Fiction

In the parking lot of a dying dream

An actor is comforted by his one true friend

His one true friend

Tells him not to cry in front of the Mexicans

Once Upon a Time in Hollywood

For Quentin Tarantino

Los Angeles

Is a town filled with Mexican extras

Quentin Tarantino writes and directs

About a city

He thinks he loves

But cannot see

Quentin Tarantino is American

And Los Angeles

Is Mexican

The second

Largest Mexican city in the world

Did know

Hidden in plain sight

Beneath plates of gold

The Oscar is a Mexican

And no one ever talks about

And isn't that just like Los Angeles

Even When We Win

Between 1974 and 2006

3 friends

Martin Scorsese

Steven Spielberg

And Francis Ford Coppola

Won a total

Of 4 Oscars

Between 2013 and 2018

3 friends

Alfonso Cuaron

Guillermo Del Toro

And Alejandro Iñárritu

Won a total of 5

And yet no one ever talks about it

Alejandro Iñárritu

Is only the second director

In the history of the academy

To win the award

Back to back

And yet when Iñárritu won his second

The orchestra played him off

And yet when he won his first

Sean Penn asked

"Who gave this son of a bitch

A green card"

Even when we win

We must be ignored

We must be disrespected

When They Speak of Crisis

In both

Breaking Bad

And Better Call Saul

Though the first much worse

White men fall from grace

Whereas Mexicans

Are born more or less criminal

In the case of the second

Some are good people

In both

The fall of basic white decency comes

From contact with the world of inherent

Mexican corruption

These shows

Modern day westerns

Same cast of heroes

Same cast of villains

Same plot points and cautionary tales

Years ago

When I was traveling

A racist young Canadian

Asked me why I didn't like the show

Breaking Bad

I said "because it's racist"

I said "because it makes Mexicans look like mindless zombies"

I pointed out the characters of the twins

Between the two of them

They didn't have a single line of dialogue

Except in childhood

I pointed out their lack of depth

I pointed out one of them

Crawled from a deathbed

With severed legs

Just to bleed out a nightmare

He said "yeah

But they're drug dealers"

I said "so is Walter White"

And he looked genuinely perplexed

When they

Speak of the opioid crisis

They speak

Of the heartland

The northeast

Or the Pacific northwest

The speak of

States with an overwhelming

White majority

No one ever talks about New Mexico

New Mexico is second only

To Massachusetts

In death per capita

Related to Fentanyl

When the speak of crisis

The victims are white

The dealers are not

Even when die

We must be ignored
We must be the villain
We must play the part

No Pigs in Vato Heaven

And I was like "bro
I hate that fucking shit
The walking dead
Season 1
Episode 4
Vatos
Check it out they are on
The run from a fucking
Zombie apocalypse
And they find a perfectly good
Functioning society
And they are like nah we're good
We'd rather take our chances
With a zombie fucking apocalypse
Than
Live under vato rule"
And he was like "nah foo
Rick's a cop
He had to go"
And was like "damn bro

You right

No pigs in vato heaven"

Fort Hollywood (A Semi True Story About a Semi Real Place Sometimes Called Los Angeles)

So I'm in Havana

And I of course

I should be enjoying

The moment

But I didn't get anywhere

By enjoying anything

And I'm speaking at a conference

On a panel at Casa de las Américas

And I am sitting here with

Living legend

The man himself

Luis Rodriguez

And I am all questions

And he is telling me about

Stabbings

Shootings

The bottle

The needle

How he wrote himself out of the Los Angeles prison

How he wrote himself out of addiction

The dungeons

They built for us

The dungeons

We built for ourselves

But no story wilder than this

Seems back in the day Hollywood

Came sniffing around

Offered him millions

To option

Always Running

I asked why he didn't take it

Said it wasn't worth it

I said "what do you mean"

He said they wanted to set the story in Hell's Kitchen

He said they wanted to make the Mexicans Irish

I said "that's crazy"

That night I had a dream

We took to the hills

Like Che and Fidel

With a rebel army

Of Writers

Directors

Best boys

And actors

And we seized Fort Hollywood

And the studios fell

And the moguls fled

And we opened the gates

And we did it big

And we did it different

We empowered the people

The people told their stories

Their stories resonated with the world

We changed the whole game

And it was a golden age

A Razasciance if you will

We kept the Oscar though

Be a shame

You know

To just throw away

A perfectly good Mexican

They Climbed Into a Graveyard

They started young

And they were the best

The best of friends

And if you weren't one of them

Well then you just wouldn't understand

And that was just as well

For life is short

The world is wide

And they were twelve

And who at that age

Has the time to explain

The mystery

The meaning

Of singing skies

Birds that cry

International code

The cosmic jest

Contraband eyes

Inside jokes

No

They grew up across the tracks

Parents went way back

But didn't get along

Well their fathers did

But their mothers didn't

And you know how that goes

Some argument

Some years ago

Didn't seem like much at the time

But like the acid

From the battery factory

Over the years

It seeped into every aspect of their lives

They lived under power lines

Rent hikes

Barbed wire

The killer's siren

Near soil that poisoned the lungs

As though the gun blast

The soundtrack

To the late eighties

Or their parents screaming through failing marriages

Was not poison enough

They resented their fathers

For how they treated their mothers

Their mothers for how they treated them

One tried to teach the other Spanish

And the other to imagine

An old Mexico

Before their time

Frozen in place

La patria

De Infante

Negrete

Gloria Marin

Maria Felix

A golden age

Of balcony and serenade

Where two weary travelers

Could finally be themselves

They worked hard

They worked smart

They stayed inside

They stayed up nights

They sacrificed

They were first generation college grads

They left the old neighborhood

And talked for years of one day giving back

They never did

They lived to see amazing things

The making of history

The Browning of America

Taco trucks on every corner

A telenovela on every screen

They shattered glass ceilings

Got jobs with bosses

Who stole their ideas

Married men

Who left them for younger women

Had children

Some who made them proud

And

Some who didn't

Though which was which

Was never hard to guess

They would only ever tell each other

And they would laugh

And laugh

And laugh

And laugh until they were done

Because laughing at the lives

That despite our best efforts

Turn out just like our parents

Is exactly what best friends are for

They fell out

Ages ago really

They didn't speak for decades

Each faced the pain of age

The gathering of graves

The golden years

Where everything finally starts clicking

When you can finally make sense

Of all this mystery and meaning

Without the ear of the one person

Who understood them best

They reconnected sometime last year

After one of their husbands finally died

Now in their late eighties

They spoke solemn at first

Of out of respect

Then laughed and mourned

The loss of their own time

And they cried

And they cried

And they cried

And they cried until they were done

Each telling the story of the other

Each telling the stories that defined their lives

And as this story nears its end

There is time yet still for one

Sometime in their late forties

They finally reached old Mexico

They dipped their toes

In two oceans

Sat at the foot of the pyramids

Their eyes drank in the mountains

As they recalled the legends of lovers

On the final day

They dressed in the glamor

Of another time

Frozen in place

They came upon a graveyard

Appearing to be locked

Undeterred

One stepped into their others palms

Once lifted she extended her arm

Helped her friend over the iron rods

They crashed to the ground

They tore their dresses

They spent hours

Searching for the grave of Maria Felix

They sat for hours

At the grave of Maria Felix

Each telling the story of the other

Of the tragedy and folly

Of having been born

In the wrong place

At the wrong time

They left the way they came in

Clawing

Across the street a child was pointing

And laughing

One cried back in her Mexican American

Accent

"Oye payaso

Que haces

Dónde está su padres"

The child laughed and said nothing

And pointed to an open door

Now they were all laughing

They had climbed into a graveyard for nothing

And yet what is a life without laughter

And yet any story worth having is worth living

And yet

Laughing at our decisions

Our regrets

At the lives we have led

Despite our best efforts

Is exactly what best friends are for

And they were the best

The very best

The best of friends

Brunch in America

It had been

A debacle

A disgrace

A fiasco

In a word

Garrulous

It had been

A trial

A tribulation

In a phrase

Four long years

And four extremely wealthy

And four extremely white liberals

Could all in unison agree

Each had done more than enough

To earn themselves a brunch

To the country club

Each hopped

Into their tesla

Made their way

To the tall all white columns

To fresh cut green

To the well manicured

All Brown staff

Just before the restaurant

Doors opened

Each peaked through a crack of light

Into the life of service

Gathered for them

An angry middle aged man

Was shouting in Spanish

Appeared ready to burst from his company suit

Seeing the servant's distress

The youngest wealthy white liberal

Cried out in bejeweled ecstasy

"Oh that's wonderful"

Hearing this

The service

Scrambled to position

The doors opened

The friends were seated

One of the wealthy white liberals

Raised questions

And it was explained

The middle aged man

Was management

An evangelical

Troubled by the results of the election

All the friends laughed

"Silly little Brown man

The fault lie not in the absence of a right wing God

But in the hands of a dread orange

And now Joe and Kamala

Have come

To set all the silly little Brown people free"

Just then

An ICE raid

Deported the entire staff

The friends were informed by

The state

They would have to find brunch elsewhere

The friends

Left the club

To find their

Favorite valet missing

Caught up in the sweep

The wealthiest lifted a rock

And in full view

Of the law

Crushed the box

Holding the driverless fobs

To the rustic road

The friends sat

In gridlocked traffic

The friends left their cars

The friends walked to the head

Of the commotion

There they saw and an officer

The friends demanded

Answers

The checkpoint was supposedly

For drivers under the influence

But the officer explained

"We're stealing cars from

The illegals"

The wealthiest white liberal

Walked to the front of the pack

Slapped the officer

"What year is this

Joe and Kamala

Are in office

Conduct your duties

Without the racial overtones"

The other wealthy white liberals

Applauded in unison

Cried out in luxurious delight

"Oh that's wonderful"

The wealthiest white liberal

Gathered the driverless fobs

Handed them to the officer

And instructed

Their Teslas be returned by mid afternoon

That in each of their windows

Read signs

"Love is love

Black lives matter

Science is real

And no one is illegal"

The friends

Walked on

Giddy in their love

Of Joe

So obviously

Decent

Giddy in their love

Of Kamala

Which was very progressive

The friends laughed

And talked

And walked

And talked

And laughed

Themselves into

An uptown stupor

They walked for miles

Until they reached

The Mexican border

Where upon they found

A wall

The youngest cried out

The dread Orange

Must have built this wall under

The cover of night

The friends demanded a the nearest agent

Drive them to the nearest protest

Upon arrival

They approached the nearest

Loud person with a megaphone

Who was a young woman

Which all the friends agreed

Was very progressive

The protest

Was at a large

Facility

Still caging children

The wealthiest white liberal told the young protester

About the wall

The protestor

Said it was built by Bill Clinton

Infuriated all the wealthy white liberals

Said the silly Brown protester was mistaken

The wealthy white liberals threw a moneyed tantrum

The wealthiest demanded answers

The murderous Brown guards

Perplexed

Called upon the white warden

The white warden

Perplexed

Cut through the crowd

As the murderous Brown guards

Beat their way through the Brown protestors

The white warden welcomed the wealthy white liberals

The white warden explained

"These are not kids in cages

These are unaccompanied minors

This is not a child prison

This is an overflow facility"

The wealthiest white liberal

Infuriated

Demanded the white warden "do better"

The wealthiest white liberal

Cried out in a flurry

"Housing fulfillment center"

Migrant child care facilities"

"Phrases that better emphasize

The temporary nature

Of the situation

The basic decency

Of Joe and Kamala

The deep commitment

They hold

To ongoing human rights"

The white warden nodded in agreement

Asked then

How to repay

This generosity

The wealthiest white liberal

Replied they had been trying for hours

Seemed like days

To go to brunch

The white warden snapped his fingers

And the murderous Brown guards

Snapped into action

A table was found

A table was set

A staff was formed

The murderous Brown guards

Scurried to service

In full view

Of caged children

The wealthy white liberals

Cried in wealthy white unison

"We would kill for mimosas"

For Mexicans Born North of Tijuana

Lost and uncertain

There is no way in

Or out

No pot to melt in

No box on the census

For Mexicans born north of Tijuana

There is no assimilation

There is only forgetting

For over amber waves of sour cream

Stale lettuce

Shredded beef

America is the great cheese grater

Between metropolises

City of angels

City of sin

The desert heat

Dries and burns the skin

Vultures hang overhead

Their caw his only companion

Buildings in the distance

Wonders if harbingers of death share in

The mirage and illusion of man

Eyes narrowing

Knees weakening

One by one

Man watches

As the vultures begin

To fall in blood

Widespread mighty wings

Blood soaked talons

Eclipsing the sun

The Eagle speaks

"Why have you abandoned our ways

For the ways of the Gachupín"

Man falls to the ground

Man begins to uncontrollably weep

"What the fuck is a gauchopin"

The Eagle screams

"A crillio

A Spaniard

A gavacho

A gringo

The white man"

Man cries back

"Oh you fucking Mexicans are all the same

I am gonna die out here

And you're giving me this shit

I was born here bro"

The eagle remains

And man cries

"What has Mexico ever done for me"

The Eagle replies

"What have you ever done for Mexico"

Man spits back

"You fucking Chicanos are all the same

What have the Chicanos ever done for me"

The Eagle replies

"What have you ever done

For the Chicanos"

Man in dust

In burning sun

Rises to his feet

Responds

"Nothing

I've done nothing

For anyone

And it is all I ask in return

Now let me die in peace"

Man presses on

Desert sun blazes

Man begins to hobble

Man's body dries

Man crashes to the dirt

Man's body jerks

Man's instincts kick in

And something stronger

Than man's will speaks

"Eagle you win

Get me out of this

And I promise

I will rededicate my life"

Man wakes in a city of lights

His body strong

"Crazy dream"

Proud Mexican Eagles

Need to call my mom"

Man thinks

And with that

Man hits the slots

The drinks are flowing

The money is spending

Once more

At a lonesome table

Dressed as a casino dealer

The Eagle cuts the deck

And says

"Live it up chamaco

For tomorrow

You become a new man"

Man laughs it off

"That was just desert talk

Eagle

Better get in line

I must pledge my life

Like

Two or three times a week"

Man left the table

Walks back to his room

And the Eagle reappears as at pit boss

"First lesson to be a great Mexican

You must be a man of your word

Un hombre de bigote"

"I told you bro

I am from here"

And man walked on

The Eagle pled

"Turn your back

Break your word

And I can no longer protect you"

"Never asked"

Spoke man

Once in his room

Self satisfied

Rolled back to sleep

In the sheets of a gambling den

Man is awoken by a low weak voice

"A survey

For your stay"

Man turns to see

A slithering snake

"Are you Mexican"

"I am from Torrance"

"Are you Chicano"

"I don't do the marching"

"Do you reject Mexico"

"I want to sleep"

"Do you reject Mexico"

"I reject Mexico"

"Of course you do

Who would ever want to be Mexican

Lazy stupid

Only good for stealing the jobs no one wants

Do you reject Chicano"

"In a heartbeat now good night"

"Of course you do

Cholos

Criminals killing and poisoning the innocent

Fake Mexicans

No culture

No homeland

Next step

Do you reject your father"

"Only when he is drinking"

"Do you reject your mother"

"Watch that shit"

"Do you reject your mother"

"You better shut the fuck up"

"Reject your mother"

And with that man leapt to his feet

"You better get the fuck out of here

Or I'm going to fuck you up

Right now motherfucker"

And with that

The snake replied

"What I do I do in self defense

Officer I feared for my life"

Then bit the ankle of man

Man fell to the ground

Man fell into a dream

Lost and uncertain

Man again wandered the desert

Until the sky turned red

And the land turned green

And all the world was a cactus

And everywhere snakes were biting

The ankles

Of eagles

Who in turn

Became snakes

Who in turn repeated the lies the slander

To the ever changing standards

The Eagle was falling

The Snake was rising

Man was surrounded

By the slithering and hissing

And all sounded

As man had sounded

His whole life

A total disgrace

Man stood in tears

As snakes placed upon him

A star spangled banner

And a baked crown of apple pie

King of the coconuts

Man woke in shame

Man knew he deserved

To have died in the desert

Man knew it was not his

But the strength

Of his people

That had lifted him

Man woke

Un hombre de bigote

A man of his word

And that man

Stands before you today

So when you are feeling

Lost and uncertain

Weak and American

I will be strong and Mexican

Enough for us both

We are proud eagles

We were born to soar

To take the sky

And how we will fly

And how we will fly

And how we will fly

And how will we fly

By not asking

A fucking snake

Narciso's Cabin

A lawyer

Of a bygone era

Invites a bickering

Intelligentsia

To his cabin

A handler

Instructs them

To surrender

Electronics

And their signatures

To an NDA

The guest list includes

A poet

A Marxist historian

A prison abolitionist

A postmodernist

An ethnic studies consultant

And a social media influencer

Their host is nowhere be seen

And there is a sense

Among them

That it will be a long weekend

The kitchen is fully equipped

The table is set

And the winter is falling

The poet makes a toast
"To this historic weekend
To our minimalist host
The US may come and go
But the Chicanos
You shall always have"
The social media influencer
Alone
Is clearly upset
But outnumbered
Says nothing
And the rest raise their glass
And the night goes on
And the Marxist
Who knows Narciso best
Tells stories of the man
The myth the legend
And the snow piles
Heavier and heavier
And Narciso is still nowhere to be found
The cabin is searched
A shriek is heard
Lying dead in his bed
In dinner attire

Narciso is found

The abolitionist

Seizes control

Instructs everyone

Not to touch the body

Instructs the

Ethnic studies consultant

To make the call

As the weeping poet is comforted

The landline is dead

The power is cut

Panic sets in

The abolitionist instructs everyone

To go their rooms

To lock their doors

Until questions can be answered

Until order

Can be restored

The following day

The abolitionist

The Marxist

The postmodernist

And the social media influencer gather around

A table

The poet is absent

The Marxist demands the poet's presence

The social media influencer

Demands space be held

For the trauma the poet must be experiencing

Deems the Marxist's demand

The Marxist's tone

The Marxist's demanding tone problematic

Literal violence

The ethnic studies consultant

Reports back the power is still cut

The abolitionist

Instructs the Marxist

To gather snow in boxes

To preserve the food

The Marxist instead

Demands that the poet

Come sit at the table

Against the protest of

Both the influencer

And postmodernist

The Marxist

Goes to the poet's room

The ethnic studies consultant

Gathers the snow

The Marxist returns

Pale and terrified

The poet is dead

An ax buried in the poet's chest

The social media influencer

Is first to respond

"Why are the poets

Always first to go"

The Marxist immediately

Questions why

The influencer did not want

The poet called to the table

The influencer responds

The Marxist was first to find the body

And that Chicanosaurs are completely problematic

The abolitionist demands

All sit at the table

The Marxist alone disagrees

And it is agreed

That Marxism is indeed

 Problematic

Toxic even

The Marxist is swarmed

Beaten

Subdued

The abolitionist

Instructs that the Marxist

Be tied to a chair

And locked in the closet

The rest gather around the table

Now safe from the Marxist

The abolitionist holds court

To decide the Marxist's fate

And contemplate

The meaning of restorative justice

The social media influencer

Warns that no one can think clearly

With all this trauma

Instructs everyone to focus

On their breathing

To stay hydrated

Asks about their sleep habits

Asks that they all self audit

Where are they marginalized

Where are they privileged

How can they do better

Reduce harm

The social media influencer

Sadly concludes

Both the abolitionist

And ethnic studies consultant

Are both problematic

Toxic even

Instructs the postmodernist

To divvy up the rations

According to the findings

And life goes on like this

And the Marxist withers in the closet

And the others wither in their rooms

The social media influencer

Instructs them

To focus on their trauma

To focus on their wounds

To focus on their breathing

While there is still time

The ethnic studies consultant

Is the first to go

Soon too, the abolitionist

Follows suit

Once confirmed dead

The postmodernist

Takes an ax

Calmly walks to the closet

The Marxist sits in contempt

The postmodernist says

"You are one tough old bastard"

Before striking the Marxist dead

The social media influencer

And postmodernist leave the cabin

Walk into the snow

On their way to meet

The handler

The social media influencer

Is giddy at

How they well they work together

At the prospect

Of the bright future that lay ahead

When an ax is buried

In the influencer's back

The influencer mutters back "why"

The postmodernist replies

"Your treachery

Only bought you time

You thought you could bring down

A movement with what

Your selfies

Self interest

Self-indulgence

You thought your ideas were your own

I created the National Endowment for Democracy

The Congress of Cultural Freedom

The Paris Review

I create my own opposition

And an ever changing language

For it to use

I work for the CIA

I get paid"

And with that

The postmodernist

Left them all dead

In the snow

The Mountain, the River, the Valley

The Mountain

Upon my travels
In my search for meaning
I came one day
Upon a poorly
Kept gate
And beyond the gate
Lay a mountain
And beyond the mountain
According to the old man
Keeping the gate
A valley
A valley of legends
And I thought perhaps
This could be
The end to my wandering
I cried to the old man
"Surely
I am worthy
Worthy of this valley
This valley of the legends
Let me pass"
"You may not"
He cried back
"For I am the keeper of the gate
And I am very wise"
I could see quickly
He could not be easily convinced
And not one for senseless conversation
I lifted a rock
And struck the old man dead
Opened the door
And headed towards the mountain
Once upon the mountain

I climbed
And I climbed
As the air thinned
Doubt formed around my steps
Could this valley
This valley of legends
Simply have been
The ramblings of a failed old man
An old failed man
I struck dead then
For no reason
It was then
A quarter of the way up
I came upon a ragged beggar
"Stop" he cried
"For I know what is you are after
And I am very wise
And with your strength
And with my mind
Surely we will reach the valley
The valley of legends"
I replied
"Old man
The mountain makes its own demands
And you would only hold me back
Slow my way"

"Wait" he cried
As he pled out a parable

(The Parable of the Track Runner)

Once there was a track runner
A poor boy
Poorly born
To a family without name
And yet with talent alone

In the shadows

And sidelines
Of those bred and poised for victory
He would routinely place
Just below medaling
To the victors went the spoils
To little Caesars
Went the withering laurels
One day
The poor boy
Left to train
On desert
On beach
Let the sand claim his feet
He pushed into darkness
Into silence

Running up the hill
All would be made right
He would be made whole
The poor boy returned to the race
Outpaced them all
Crossed the finish line
Fell into heap and began to cry
When he opened his eyes
He was back in the stands
Watching the ceremony

And now the tears
Rolled down my face
As the wise man said
That which he need not explain
"And the moral of this story is this
We can do everything
This world demands
And still be cheated"
"Yes" I cried
"You are very wise"
And with that
I lifted him upon my back

And together we carried on

Further up the mountain

Upon our climb
The wise man was full of life and wonder
Depth and humor
Humanity and splendor
Grateful was he to be carried up the mountain
Grateful was he to be carried
That much closer to the valley
But as we climbed on
Soon enough though his wisdom soured
As he began to recount
All the ways in life he had been cheated
A familiar song
And it was then I asked

The old man
How he had come to hear of this valley
And it was then he confessed
He too had once kept the gate
And it was then that I questioned

For how many years

And it was then that I questioned

How much time he had wasted

And it was then that I questioned
The value of a man
Twice my age
Who had only come half as far
And sensing what was coming
A wise man indeed
He sunk his teeth

Into my back
Just before I shook the old hater
Towards his rocky death
And I stared towards the top of the mountain

I thought "that final bite
Was the only mark
That man will have ever left"
I climbed on till I reached the summit
At the mountains summit
There stood yet another man claiming wisdom
It appeared he had been waiting a long time
But he did not plea
And he did not cry
He spoke instead in command
"Hear now
My parable
The Parable of gorgeous George and Ugly Pete"

(The Parable of Gorgeous George and Ugly Pete)

Once there was a town
And in this town
Two beggars
Gorgeous George and Ugly Pete
Humble in pain
Malnourished
Ugly Pete
Languished on the wretched vine of charity
While Gorgeous George the apple
Of the town's eye
Ate from the vast plane of adoration
Gorgeous George
Shoes unwiped
Would enter homes
Slap the face of the eldest son
And sit in the father's chair
As he was fanned and fed grapes
Starving and alone
Ugly Pete left town
And on that day

The strangest thing happened

The years rushed upon

Gorgeous George's face
The town filled with rage and hate
A cry went out
And the hearts of a boiling mob hardened
Gorgeous George
Gorgeous no more
Murdered
Drawn and quartered
His bones scattered
In the town square
And after the carnage
After catharsis
The strangest thing happened
A collective sadness came over the town
Feelings of guilt and shame
For the decades of mistreatment
Of poor Ugly Pete
Signs went up
Search parties went out
But all that was found
Were his withering remains
The town cried
And statue was built in the main square
Over the unmarked grave
Of the once Gorgeous George
A monument
To the eternally Ugly Pete
Pride of the town
And patron saint of the wretched

And when the tale was done the wise man said
"And the moral of this story is"
But before he could finish
I kicked him square in his chest
And as he fell from the mountain peak

I asked "do a I look like a beggar to you"

And now
I began the mountain's descent
And the air was thin and the wind was cruel
And I was alone
Alone
Alone
The world alone
It shatters the spirit
It weakens the bones
Why must such journeys as this
Always be waged alone
I journeyed on
And came upon
A welcoming cry
"Come in come in"

Came out of a cave torch lit
They cried in committee
The air was warm and thick
And filled with community
The air was warm and thick
And filled with poetry
I listened in

You know what
Maybe this is about you
And 1492

Beat you for begging
Beat you for sleeping
Beat you for breathing

You will travel
You will live
And the star lit skies were his
And the open plains
The cityscapes

"Wait" I cried

"These poems
Are mine"
"Yes" they cried
"Today is the day
We honor the poet laureate of the cave"
"But these poems
These poems are mine
"Yes it is you
You are the poet laureate of the cave"
They cried
Tears filled my eyes
As I was led to sit upon a throne
As I cried
"Could it be true"
Ancient laurels were placed upon my head
My praises were sung
Fanned and fed grapes
"Yes" I cried "this will be a wonderful tale
To tell the others
Once I reach the valley
The valley of the legends"
"No need"
They cried
"You are home
You are the poet laureate of the cave"
And it was then I could feel the strength leaving my legs
Under the weight
Of withering laurels
"No" I cried
As I ran my way back
Through a symphony
Of my own poetry
Out the mouths of angels
I threw down the flames
To set fire to the cave
I pushed a rock
Over it's entrance
So none might tempt my return

Tears in my eyes
 I cried
"I do not any of want this"
As I thought of Gorgeous George
And Ugly Pete

I cried

As I wondered
Whether the parable was truth
"Are only hacks celebrated in life
Are the true artists only ever realized in death
And if so

Where then does my art stand`
Which one am I"
More uncertain than I when I began
I headed on down towards the foot of the mountain

The River

At the foot of the mountain
There lies a river
And in the river
There stood my mother
"Mother"
I cried
As I waded into the water
"Mother I killed so many people
To reach this valley
This valley of the legends
Mother even if it is a lie
Tell me it is real
Tell me they did not die in van"
"How dare you"

Cried back my mother in scorn
"How dare you
Take full credit for all the blood you have shed
When it was I who gave you life

When it was I who gave you strength"
I hung my head in shame
"Mother all I ever wanted
In life was to be loved
And then not love in return
Is that too much to ask"
"Insatiable child
Earn your keep
Take this dagger
It is for your father
Beyond him
Lies the valley
This valley of the legends
That you seek"
I waded on and on
And on

And on
And began to wither
Fatigue made coward
Preparing myself
To die in the river
To smile at how far I had come
When pair of strong arms
Carried me to shallow waters
Once my legs were under me
My father's arms opened
As he welcomed fate
And I asked myself
Does this thing
This valley
This valley of legends
Mean so much to me
That I would bury a dagger in my father's chest
Yes
But when the blade stabbed him
The knife became a plastic

Retractable toy

And everywhere I stabbed at him
A wound would appear on me
And even knowing this
I could not stop myself from stabbing
Bloodied and now dying

Once more I fell into
Into the arms of my father
Tears in his eyes
"Son, the blade was never for me
It was always for you"
And with that he vanished
And so did my wounds
With no further instruction
I trailed down the river
Filled with resolve and determination
I met my final obstacle
I met myself
And I asked "are you here to kill me"
I cried back

"No
I am here to baptize you"
I asked "what's the difference"
I lunged and fought myself to the death
Held my head under the water
As I cried
"Deserve
Deserve
Deserve"
Until the word lost all meaning

Until I stood over myself
And emerged

From the river baptized and worthy

Worthy of this valley
This valley of the legends

The Valley

Once in the valley
My feet left the ground
I began to float
Told
In the valley of legends
We rise and fall
Advance and retreat
On the wings of memory
Years passed just like this
Ebb and flow
Back and forth
Always further forward then backwards
Years to decades
And my heart swelled with thought of centuries
Until one day
Weary I came upon a gate
Rested against it's door
Days became weeks
Weeks

Decades
And I gathered dust
Content now in my legend
Until I saw a young man
Far young than I
When I first reached this valley
And as he approached
I saw the young man was swimming through the sky

I was never told you could swim through the sky
I said to the young man

"Young man where are you headed"
He cried back
"Rest easy old legend
I am headed to the valley of the immortals"
I was never told there was a valley of the immortals
And for the first time
I looked beyond the gate

And beyond the gate
There was another mountain
And I imagined beyond
The mountain
A valley
And I cried out
"Wait young I very wise
And with your strength
And my mind
Surely we can reach this valley
This valley of the immortals"
The young man cried back
"Old man if I could use you
You would be there by now
Do not fret old legend
You did well"
Desperate to prove my value
I began to cry out a parable

(The Parable of the Poet Laureate of the Cave)

Once there was a poet
Who came upon a cave

But not one for senseless poetry or parables
The young man struck a stone against my head
I crashed to the ground
My blood on the gate
Spilling around me
I stared out into distance
At yet another mountain
With the promise of yet another valley
With my arm extended
With my final breath
Grasping for immortality

Bad Hombre/Way of the Jaguar/ FlowerStrong/The Architect's Daughter/Clowns on the Internet/San Diego Vs In Lak'Ech/A Very Formal, Very Official Legal Application to Make March 4th a National Chicano Holiday/Grito

Bad Hombre

I am Zorro

Machete

The Cisco kid

Anthony Quinn

Cutting the bullet

From his own leg

That which

You struggle to name

But still lives in your head

A Mexican standoff

And Montezuma's revenge

I am one bad hombre

Way of the Jaguar

The Way of the Jaguar

Is the way of the

Intercepting fact

The Jaguar is not

Here to critique

Deconstruct

Interrogate

The metaphor or identity

Of a postmodern

Postcolonial imaginary

No, no the Jaguar has no

Time for that

The way of the Jaguar

Is scientific

Dialectic

Canta no llores

Smile now

And cry never

The Way of the Jaguar

Is door to door

Pound the pavement

Fight the fascists

Build the organization

And as the world goes viral

The Jaguar can fight there too

The Jaguar has no compassion

And asks no compassion of you

The Jaguar is not love

The Jaguar is a hammer

Used to crush its enemies

And while history might not

Absolve the Jaguar

When our time comes

The Jaguar will not apologize

For the memes

FlowerStrong

Los Angeles to Tucson

Tucson to Dallas

Dallas to Houston

Houston to Austin

Austin to San Anto

San Anto to Burque

Y Burque back to El Lay

Four days

All clout no chase

Poets

Authors

Authorized vendors

Independent contractors

Road warriors

Of the event listing

The press release

Industry men

Who cross their T's

Who dot their I's

Quick with the W9

Stone cold killers

Who roll up their sleeves

And get it right

And even then

Still might not get paid on time

But they don't tweet

And they don't cry

Because internet tears

Are only good for internet likes

Not return business

And these seasoned vets

Are all about theirs

Handsome devils

Who live out of suitcases

And pack their dreams in the carry on

Never leave them far behind

Cause once off the plane

You can never go back

And that is that

The song of the road

The hustler's code

Same as it ever was

FlowerSong

FlowerStrong

The Architect's Daughter

The paved hills

The potted trees

The steel and concrete

That tumble between

Full bright moon

Electric skyline

The poet's eyes

Could not help but

Dart and drift

Sway and swim

Between

Days and miles

Childhood

And nearby Hillside Village

Brick and dirt lot

Barbed wire and a young kid

Who could not know then

How the decrying of walls

Would come to define his life

Rooftop view

Full bright moon

City Terrace at night

The poet could not help

But recall

The memory of her father

The architect

The man who built the house she grew up in

Half dream

Half plan

Says she is saving her pennies

Says she is buying land

Says building is in the blood

Then anger she speaks

Of human need

Hidden cities

Greased palms

The real power

Of real Estate

Of real villains

With real names

Who wash their hands

In art galleries

And mayoral campaigns

City Terrace at night

Electric skyline

Rooftop view

Two poets

With empty pockets

And full hearts

Chart

A cartography of verse

Rebuild a cash torn city

Using nothing but their words

Blades to wires

Hammers to walls

It could all

Be so simple

Put the people

Without homes

In the homes

Without people

Full bright moon

Roof top view

Electric skyline

City Terrace at night

Clowns on the internet

I saw the best

Minds of my generation

Cyberbullied into submission

By clowns on the internet

Who cited first hand

Experience

To go unquestioned

But failed to mention

It was to the right

By clowns on the internet

Who donned the mask

Of the left

Only to cite the minutemen

Clowns on the internet

Cloaked in decolonization

But who proudly served

To the US war machine

Clowns

Clowns

Clowns everywhere

San Diego Vs In Lak'Ech

And now I'd like to tell you

How it all went down

What was lost in the fire

Washed away in the flood

How we never really recovered

From the big one

But

That's not what

Happened

Our disaster was man made

Ever since the invader set foot

On the continent

They banned books

Vetoed curriculum

Threw children in a barn

And said they weren't college material

We fought back

We walkout

We sit in

We Mendez

We Lemon Grove

We Acosta vs Huppenthal

They San Diego vs In Lak'Ech

In San Diego

A group of racist

Parents sued the school

District

For the teaching of the poem

In Lak'Ech

They said it promoted

The values

Human sacrifice

And cannibalism

After all these years

They're still

Calling us savages

What's wrong with these people

A Very Formal, Very Official Legal Application to Make March 4th a National Chicano Holiday

Hear me out

They got to Cinco De Mayo

And are quickly ruining

Dio De Los Muertos

But no way will Disney or Coors

Will touch this one

Let's make March 4th

A National Chicano holiday

We'll call it

The fall of the Alamo

No we'll call it

We stabbed Davy Crocket

As Jim Bowie hid under his bed crying

Day

Picture

Pilgrimages

To San Antonio

By the busload

Picture singing loud Spanish songs

Half of us don't know the words too

We will wear futbol jerseys

Of Mexican teams

That we will pretend

We have supported

Our whole lives

As long as they say Mexico

Somewhere on them

When we get there

We will pass out

Large foam fingers

That say we're number one

Viva México Cabrones

Grito

And now I would

Like to tell you about

Some of my friends

Thes sons and daughters

The daughters and sons

Of plumbers

Bus drivers

Drywall installers

File clerks

Field hands

And highwaymen

Who stood before whiteboards

Of power

Who pressed

Opinion to paper

Who professed sociology

Who flung freed time

At utility knives

And wood varnish

Who chaired departments

Professed history

Who skewered

The rat mascot

Of 20th century

Who debated esteemed Jesuits

Through hallowed halls

Presumed incompetent

Carrying six languages

Over five continents

Fresh as the lettuce

Who walked the bright light

Famed and obscure

Toured thirty four states

Chasing the glory road

Of his famed uncle

Who dedicated his work

To the living memory

Of his working father

Who pondered what the pavement

Took from his grandfather's hands

Who evoked the ghost

Of Posada

Against the dead dreams

Of capital

Who commissioned

The writing on the wall

Whose pen uncovered

The lies of nations

Who took up the banner

Of revolution

Who wrote a letter to his son

That shaped a field of study

Who shouldered the legacy

Of family

Who carried the banner of

Self determination

Who penned

The banned curriculum

The forbidden words .

Who stood trial on principle

Who received

Slander

Death threats

For attempts

To teach oncoming generations

The basic truths of the murderous country

Who born of the outskirts

To military tradition

Who once held the rifle of empire

Who climbed the ivory tower

Who walked the picket line

Who heard the cry of the colonies

Who put them down in ink

Who crossed borders

For a concert

Only to build a career

En la frontera

Who studied at the finest schools

The yankees had to offer

Only to point out their failures

Who learned a craft

For a job

Only to make a life of Mosaic

Who taught in the prisons

Only to be threatened by the state

Who took up the banner

Of Mexican culture

Only to be slandered

By the jealous

Corrupt and unprincipled

Who covered a city in tile

Who covered a city in stone

In celebration of those

Who built it's imagination

Who fought the lies of a school district

Who recovered the sacred

The indigenous root

From the working fields

Of Oxnard

Who recovered

The past from the cell

At Los Padrinos

Who brought light

To school to prison pipeline

Who instructed the teachers

Out in Chicago

On ways of being

Who hauled canvases and prints

Through the Cajon Pass

Whose imagery evoked the past

In pursuit of a dream

Who climbed the wooden attic

Of the once tallest building

Of Los Angeles

Who cycled the metropolis

Mining the street

The sky

For the secret fortune

Of the hidden city

Buried in plain sight

Who found redemption

In paint and canvas

Who sketched his vision

Across the skyline of his birth

Who painted the classic

Out of the world around him

Who occupied Los Angeles

Who staged a tree protest

Who published voices

Across continents

Who lived in a liberated

Army barracks in Bari

Who lived above

Shakespeare and Company

A vagabond

Against empire

Who as a boy watched the work ethic

Of a single mother

Then wrote out a life

A poet

A publisher

A latch key kid

Who worked

And worked

And worked

To build the most

Prolific Brown press of all time

Who was driven from the halls

Of academia

Into the bars

The cafes

Bellowing

Bella Ciao

The Internationale

Who translated the voices

Of the proletariat

Who marched the streets

Of San Francisco

A proud Marxist Leninist

Who decried

The proud city of San Francisco

With National Union of the Homeless

Who spoke against

The school of the Americas

Who spoke in solidarity

With the Sandinistas

Over Soviet airwaves

Whose voice

Whose fire

Whose syntax

In mysterious order

Traveled the world

Crossed the ocean

Who was solicited

By the stuff of dreams

By the coveted print

Who was hailed

By the greatest living historian

As the premier

Revolutionary poet of the day

Who read in the living rooms

Of legends

Whose legend grew

With the contemplation

Of four walls

Who wrote of

Photographs and prison letters

And the themes of the universe

Who I met in a basement

When we were both no one

Reading to audience of none

Who hopped on flights

With the hopes of freeing kids from cages

Who sat in protest

Who walked concert halls

Who threw his platform

At the primary contradiction

Who held the sword of Simon Bolivar

While staring into the eyes of Hugo Chavez

Who made the Koch brothers famous

Who was sued by Tony Blair

Who was sued by George W. Bush

Who was personally hated by Donald Trump

Who was personally hated by Hillary Clinton

Who exposed the suppression of the vote

Who exposed the crimes of the banks

Who exposed the crimes of oil

Who studied under Ginsberg

Who drank with Bukowski

Who won awards

Won by Oscar Wilde

Won by Johnathan Swift

Who called me

Yes me

The best political poet in America

Who ran with that shit

Who marketed it everywhere

Who told everyone

Who would listen

Twice if they wouldn't

Who spoke in 12 countries

3 continents

Translated and published

In seven languages

Who had a laurel placed

On his head by Franciscan monks

Twenty feet from the tomb

Of Dante Alighieri

Who walked the Malecon

Who performed on the same stage

Once graced

By Subcomandante Marcos

Who read poetry by the office of Roque Dalton

Who spoke at Cambridge

And accused the staff of being

NATO intellectuals

Who read on the same stage

Where Kissinger

Rumsfeld

And Cheney

All once stood

And it smelled of sulfur still

Who tried to scheme

His way to speak at UNAM

Only to find his book

Had beaten him there

Who walked to the edge of Venice

Contemplating only haters

Wondering if the hero

Of every story

Is the villain of another

Who summoned the past

Within his beating chest

Walking the immortal trail of Cuactemoc's

Final steps

In the living city of Tepito

Who spoke at Chicano

Youth conference

Who told the kids

My name

My name is Matt Sedillo

And that name

Means something

Because I made it

Who managed a Big 5

Chasing open mics

Off the night shift

Who begged to get on the list

Whose words took him across the world

Who had been hailed

As the best political poet in America

Not the best Hispanic

Not the best Latino

Not the best Mexican American

But the best period

Who beat his chest

Proud as hell

To be Mexican

Who beat his chest

Proud as hell

To be Chicano

Who told a youth conference

In this country that hates us

Degrades us

Aims to strip us of dignity

At every turn

I owe it to all of you

To work

And work

And work

As I hard as I can

To be the very best

At what I do

Now look around you

You owe it to each other

You owe it to your families

Your ancestors

Your descendants

Matter of fact

Fuck that

You owe it to me

To do the same

Yolqui

And this all of course

Long before

The honors

The accolades

The awards

The X

In La Raza

Tucson

Teotihuacan

Long before

Anyone

Dared

Declare

War

On the word

Chicano

And our hero

Had not yet died

No our story does

Not begin

In death

Bloodshed

With a life sentence

A police beating

Columbus

The signing of a treaty

The fall of Tenochtitlan

At the tip of a blade

The barrel of a gun

The end of a noose

As we are told so very many

Of our stories

So often do

No

Our story

Begins

Under a different sun

By a sacred mountain

With an ant

A seed

And the refusal of a god

Cintli

The corn

Yolqui

A spirit warrior

Arisen from the dead

Now this

Went down

On Whittier

Sometime after

The attack on the zoot suit

Sleepy Lagoon

The murder of Salazar

And our hero

Was a young man still

A photographer

Lowrider Magazine

He sees

The cars

The lights

The night

The Blvd

Shine electric

He sees a young man

Beaten by the police

Rushes over

And becomes the story

The sheriffs

The conquest

The banned books

The burned codices

The border walls

The prison system

The weight of history

Falls upon his head

Charges

Of assault

On an officer

Of the peace

With a camera lens

How these beasts

Must fear their

Own reflection

In Lak'Ech

I am the other you

Pancha Be

To seek the truth

Dr Cintli

Would later write

Of the beating

I died that night

How it seems death

Has its way

Of interrupting our story

Dr Cintli

Would spend the rest

Of his life

Counting the fallen

Untangling statistics

Studying maps

Against

The no

The not

The never

Of settler colonial

Scholarship

Settler colonial scholarship

That would deny

Our sacred connection

Our precious knowledge

Our science and mathematics

Dr. Cintli

Would fight all of this

In the spirit

Of a young man

Who once sat

Atop a pyramid

Stared into the distance

Our story begins

When time was still young

And the world still new

So new

That people could

Still not yet move

Quetzalcoatl

Tasked

To feed them

Searched

High and low

Land and sea

The sky and beyond

When the god met

An ant

Carrying a seed

The ant refused

"The people will bring

Their markets

Their prisons

Their borders

And from them make war

And from the corn

Poison"

But these ways are not ours

And we have work to be done

A continent to restore

And a story to tell

One where Tonatzin

Leads the East LA Walkouts

Where Popocatépetl and Iztaccíhuatl

Come down from their mountain

On the day of their wedding

Join the Moratorium

Where Nezahualcoyotl

Inspires generations

With a poem

At a youth conference in Denver

Where death has no reach

And time has no measure

Where the blood of our ancestors

Sheds our skin

Transforms us back

Back

Back into all we have ever been

So wherever they cage us

Kill us

Unmark our graves

Only to bury us in statistics

Wherever they portray us

As demons and savages

Wherever our work

Is there to be done

There

Yolqui

You will find

So roll up your sleeves

And dry your eyes

Cintli lives

And the past has not died

No the past

Has not died

No the past
Has not died
No the past
Never dies

Nos Vemos (A Meteor the Size of Texas Headed Straight For Dodger's Stadium)

One eighty

Three Sixty

Full cab

Acid drop

Anchor grind

The break of dawn

LA River is a half

Pipe

Young and old

New and semi pro

Catch air

Like it will be the last

On the day a meteor

The size of Texas

Was due to hit

Dodger's stadium

The buses still ran on time

Los compas lined up at five

Someone had to keep

The city running

On the afternoon

A meteor the size of Texas

Was due to hit Dodger's Stadium

There was a car show

In El Monte

A ceremony in Azusa

An open mic

In Boyle Heights

Where a famed poet

Who had been drinking all week

Shared most beloved poem

One last time

Formerly Brooklyn

The poet

Pointed to the street

And said

"See that

See that

That aint Chavez

That's Brooklyn

That's Brooklyn

Where's Brooklyn at

I love all of you

I will defend you

We're the best

We'll never get smoked"

Over in El Sereno

Off Huntington

There will be a roundtable discussion

Between taggers

And muralists

About the current state of affairs

In public art

And it will be a hot one

Fingers wagging

Neither side conceding

Nothing

From Laguna

To Salazar

In the heart of East Los

A protest and march

The crowd will chant

El pueblo si

La meteor no

El pueblo si

La meteor no

El pueblo

Unido

Jamas sera vencido

El pueblo

Unido

Jamas sera vencido

On the night a meteor

The size of Texas was due

Straight for Dodger's stadium

That night there will be a kick back

In Lincoln Heights

A battle of the bands in Montebello

An underground noise show

And film screening at Evergreen

A wine tasting and murder mystery

In Elysian Park

Claiming to have the best view in town

But everybody knows that's

That rooftop party in City Terrace

But the biggest thing going by far

Is a quinceañera

And concert

On the sixth street bridge

Rancheras

Cumbias

Hip hop

K pop

Reggaeton

Cholo goth

Rock en espanol

Something for everyone

And of course the cops

The cops tried to shut it down

And the people broke out into protest

Crash the barricades

Aqui estamos

Y no nos vamos

Aqui estamos

Y no nos vamos

And as the meteor closes in

The people turn their eyes

And fists to the sky

El pueblo unido

Jamas sera vencido

El pueblo unido

Jamas sera vencido

Strong and defiant

Until the very last

Until we meet again

El pueblo unido

Jamas sera vencido

El pueblo unido

Jamas sera vencido

Aqui estamos

Y no nos vamos

Aqui estamos

Y no nos vamos

Nos vemos

Andale

Let's go

I love all of you

We're the best

We'll never get smoked

Described as "The Best Political Poet in America" Matt Sedillo is the winner of the 2017 Joe Hill Poetry Labor Award and the 2022 Dante's Laurel. Sedillo is the National Coordinator for the World Poetry Movement in the US, the Literary Director of the Mexican Cultural Institute of Los Angeles, the host of Radio La Raza on KPFK 9.07 and Co Founder of El Martillo Press. Sedillo has been translated into Spanish, Italian, Hungarian, Chinese, Serbian, Farsi, Hindi and French. Sedillo has shared his work in Mexico, Canada, Cuba, Colombia, France, Italy, the UK, Hungary, Spain and Serbia. Sedillo has been featured in the Los Angeles Times, Axios, the Associated Press, La Jornada, NPR, CSPAN and various other news organizations.

FLOWERSONG
P R E S S